FALKLANDS WAR

WAR

April to June 1982

First published in July 2018

A catalogue record for this book is available from the British Library.

ISBN 978 1 78521 185 0

Library of Congress control no. 2018935486

Published by Haynes Publishing,
Sparkford, Yeovil, Somerset BA22 7JJ, UK.
Tel: 01963 440635
Int. tel: +44 1963 440635
Website: www.haynes.com

Haynes North America Inc.,
859 Lawrence Drive, Newbury Park,
California 91320, USA.

Printed in Malaysia.

Senior Commissioning Editor: Jonathan Falconer
Copy editor: Michelle Tilling
Proof reader: Penny Housden
Indexer: Peter Nicholson
Page design: James Robertson

Acknowledgements

The author would like to thank the many people who have assisted in the research and production of this book. Sincere thanks go to all the Falklands veterans who gave me their time and insight during interviews, specifically former SBS soldier 'Baz', Captain John Rees, RN, and former Marines Mark Crawford and Andy Cole, the latter who also graciously provided some superb photographs from his personal collection. My gratitude also goes to Nicci Pugh (QARNNS nurse) and Lieutenant Commander David Morgan DSC, for their permission to reprint extended passages of their memories. My thanks also go to Dave Reynolds of the Defence Picture Library, for sourcing the bulk of the photographs for this volume, and to Jonathan Falconer of Haynes Publishing, for his support during the final stages of the writing. I would also like to thank Michelle Tilling, for her careful editing.

FALKLANDS WAR

April to June 1982

Operations Manual

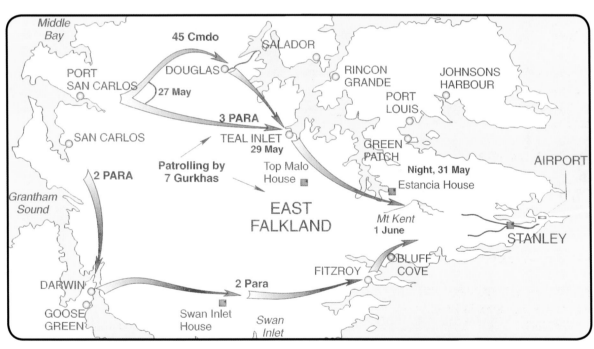

Insights into the planning, logistics and tactics that led to the successful retaking of the Falkland Islands in 1982

Chris McNab

Contents

OPPOSITE **Crammed with 3,300 military personnel, the Cunard liner RMS** *Queen Elizabeth 2* **leaves Southampton for the South Atlantic on 12 May 1982, having been requisitioned as a British troopship during the Falklands War.** *(JDHC Archive/Getty Images)*

Introduction

The Falklands War was a defining event in modern British history, socially, culturally and militarily. Although the UK had been involved in several conflicts since the end of the Second World War in 1945 – Korea, Suez, Malaysia, Cyprus, Aden, Northern Ireland – much of the practical operational experience by the early 1980s related to small-unit counter-insurgency. The Falklands would not be this sort of conflict.

In contrast to counter-insurgency ops, the training emphasis of the British armed services, especially within the NATO context, tended to be focused upon the apocalyptic scenarios of a third world war between the West and the communist USSR. Thus the war gaming and training was skewed towards countering massed Soviet armour and mechanised infantry rolling through central Europe, all conducted under the crackling pillars of atomic mushroom clouds.

Yet despite, or indeed because of, the endlessly disquieting possibilities of nuclear war, plus the perennial desire to make economic savings, the British Army, Royal Navy and Royal Air Force just prior to the Falklands War were under the spotlight for possible cuts. In June 1981, the Secretary of State for Defence, John Nott, released his report *The United Kingdom Defence Programme: The Way Forward*. In this document, Nott explained two core reasons behind the 'need for change', setting the case for rationalising and reducing Britain's armed forces against a backdrop of 'economic recession':

First, even the increased resources we plan to allocate cannot adequately fund all the force structures and all the plans for their improvement we now have. One reason (not peculiar to Britain) is cost growth,

especially in equipment. Our forces need to be equipped, operated, trained and sustained to the standards imposed by the mounting Soviet effort and the increasing sophistication of weapons. Our current force structure is however too large for us to meet this need within any resource allocation which our people can reasonably be asked to afford. [. . .]

The second reason for change, partly related to the first, concerns balance within the programme. Technological advance is sharply changing the defence environment. The fast-growing power of modern weapons to find targets accurately and hit them hard at long ranges is increasing the vulnerability of major platforms such as aircraft and surface ships. To meet this, and indeed to exploit it, the balance of our investment between platforms and weapons needs to be altered so as to maximise real combat capability.[1]

What is clear from the first of these reasons is that Britain was squarely facing east towards the Soviets in terms of its future military thinking. Such is why the defence review proclaimed that the UK government would largely maintain the force strength of the British Army of the Rhine (BAOR) at 55,000 men, although in negative balance it had originally intended to increase the manpower deployment, plus it was to

'reorganise' the four BAOR armoured divisions down to three. But elsewhere there were worrying cuts. Overall manpower levels were to be reduced – the Royal Navy was to lose 8,000–10,000 personnel, the Army 7,000 and the RAF 2,500. The Royal Navy came in for particular attention – 'A rather smaller but modern fleet with less heavy overheads will give better value for defence resources.'[2] While investment in nuclear-powered attack submarines (SSNs) was to increase, the carrier *Hermes* was to be phased out, nine destroyers and frigates were to be withdrawn, as were four Royal Fleet Auxiliary (RFA) vessels. The Royal Marines were to be maintained at present levels, but 'It had already been decided that likely needs did not warrant

replacement of the specialist amphibious ships *Intrepid* and *Fearless*; and these ships will now be phased out earlier, in 1982 and 1984 respectively.'[3] What was clear by these cuts was that Britain's ability to conduct expeditionary warfare was being seriously reduced.

Although the Nott defence cuts had not been fully rolled out by the time the Argentines invaded South Georgia and the Falkland Islands in March/April 1982, their intention does go some way to explaining the shock exhibited in confronting a new and largely unexpected threat in the South Atlantic. Veterans repeatedly talk of the sheer confusion and improvisation that came in mounting the campaign. With just days' notice, the British armed forces had to recalibrate their strategic thinking and rationalise their resources for a major infantry war 8,000 miles (12,900km) from home. Suddenly, the fullest spectrum of naval assets became critical; three of the ships noted above – *Hermes*,

BELOW The Chiefs of Staff Committee gather around a conference table in Whitehall at the height of the Falklands conflict. Chief of the Defence Staff Admiral of the Fleet Sir Terence Lewin is on the left. *(Press Association)*

Intrepid and Fearless – would actually play utterly central roles in the eventual British victory. This would not be a clash of main battle tanks (MBTs) and strategic bombers over the central European plains, but a war of small arms, light infantry and carrier/naval aviation, fought over a small, climatically hostile landscape. Had the full spectrum of the Nott cuts been implemented, it is arguable whether the British could have mounted the operation at all.

During one of my interviews for this book, an SBS veteran ('Baz') tellingly described the Falklands conflict as the 'last infantry war'. Although the recent wars in Afghanistan and Iraq have seen many infantry clashes, Baz does make an important point for reflection. The Falklands War ground campaign was largely decided by infantry from two conventional forces on an open battlefield, with limited (although critically important) artillery and air support, and mostly without the complications of a civilian presence. In the air, British Sea Harriers engaged Argentine Air Force jets in low-level dogfighting, while at sea the Navy fought its own intensive battles against anti-ship

ABOVE HMS Hermes, seen here just after the Falklands War, was slated to be phased out just prior to the onset of hostilities. Had that occurred, there is a question mark over whether Britain could have fought the conflict at all, at least in the air. (Jonathan Falconer collection)

bombing runs and Exocet strikes. Isolated at the end of their extreme journey down south, the British armed services fought a regular war very much on its own, without the enfolding support of a large coalition.

This book is not a retelling of the Falklands campaign – there are many such titles, some of the best of which are listed in the Bibliography – although the text will naturally hang upon the progression of the events. Instead, each chapter will attempt to analyse the unique set of operational, and human, factors that determined the outcome of the campaign, including tactics, logistics, intelligence, equipment, force strength, training and mobility. Whether the Falklands conflict was the 'last infantry war' is open to debate. What is not open to discussion is that, for the British, it was a war they began with highly uncertain outcomes.

Chapter One

The tactical challenge

The nature of any military campaign is often dictated by the terrain, climate and geographical extent of a military theatre or operational landmass. The physical characteristics of a war zone affect every aspect of planning, from the very clothes that individual service personnel wear through to the movements troops describe in battle. In this regard, the Falkland Islands were uniquely demanding.

OPPOSITE This panoramic view of the Falklands coastline typifies the islands' landscape, with numerous sheltered bays and inlets (although not all accessible to major vessels) and with a largely treeless and windswept interior. *(Defence Picture Library)*

The Falkland Islands sit at the extreme southern end of the South Atlantic, at a distance of 8,000 miles (12,900km) from the United Kingdom, but just 440 miles (708km) east of the Argentine mainland. The Antarctic Circle begins 850 miles (1,365km) to the south. The operational implications of this location are apparent from just a cursory glance at a map. If Britain were to fight a war here, it would have to ship everything required – men, ammunition, vehicles, helicopters, aircraft, supplies, etc. – across thousands of miles of unbroken ocean and operate in a largely self-sufficient mass without the benefits of proximate and possibly dependable resupply. Even the longest-ranged British bomber aircraft – the surviving Vulcan and Victor 'V-bombers' – could not make the journey without multiple and complex refuelling; thus air cover and Close Air Support (CAS) would have to come from carrier-based fixed-wing aircraft, plus whatever maritime or Army rotary assets could be deployed on and from ships. There was also the issue of time. It would take the British Task Force just over three weeks to sail from the UK via Ascension Island to the Falklands theatre. The positive side to this factor is that it gave time for the forces to gather intelligence, prepare troops and equipment, combat-load supplies and generally get ready – as far as possible – for what lay ahead. On the downside, it also gave the enemy an extensive window in which to prepare

defences and make tactical decisions; as we shall see, the Argentines invested heavily, but not always wisely, in readying their troops for action as the Task Force approached.

The long-distance challenges of deploying to and fighting in the Falklands could, for the British, have been insurmountable were it not for the 34-square mile (88km²) territory of Ascension Island, situated in the mid-Atlantic roughly equidistant between the eastern extremities of Brazil and the west coast of Africa around Angola, sitting just below the equator and 4,200 miles (6,800km) from Britain. A volcanic island formed out of the mid-Atlantic ridge, Ascension Island became a British possession, administered by the Royal Navy, in the 19th century, and from the 1920s was developed to assist transatlantic military and civilian logistics, both air and maritime. The island's single runway – Wideawake Airfield in the south – was developed and operated by US contractors under licence for operation by Pan American, and had a fortuitous length of 10,000ft (3,048m), sufficient for landing the largest military supply aircraft. Maritime logistics were facilitated – although limited by a single jetty – by the anchorage at Clarence Bay on the west of the island, near the capital Georgetown, and English Bay to the north. As diminutive as Ascension Island is, it was developed at speed to handle a remarkable volume of logistical traffic for the Falklands war effort (see Chapter 2).

OPPOSITE One of Britain's Type 42 destroyers cuts through the waves on exercise. At the time of the Nott defence cuts, the Type 42s formed the backbone of the UK surface warfare fleet. *(Defence Picture Library)*

LEFT The Royal Navy's nuclear submarine fleet was its greatest force for global power projection, able to sustain operations for months at a time in the most distant corners of the planet. *(Defence Picture Library)*

In contrast to the British situation, the Argentines enjoyed comparatively straightforward proximity to the islands, making the naval transfer of men and supplies relatively dependable, at least until the British imposed the Maritime Exclusion Zone (MEZ) and then Total Exclusion Zone (TEZ) around the islands. Even then, however, the Argentines had the undeniable advantage of being able to deploy combat aircraft direct from a number of Fuerza Aérea Argentina (FAA) and naval Comando Aviación Naval Argentina (CANA) air bases on the mainland. There were no fewer than five air bases within 600 miles (967km) of the Falklands, within the combat radius of most of its aircraft. Yet for all the proximity of the Falklands when compared to the British trek across the Atlantic, the distances were still not insubstantial. The range of an A-4C Skyhawk, for example, was around 2,000 miles (3,219km), so while it could certainly encompass the Falklands in its operational range, its loiter time was limited, plus its access to afterburner was restricted if it didn't want to run the risk of running out of fuel on the way home. So range was also an issue for the Argentines, and from a tactical viewpoint perhaps more so than the British once the British Task Force was deployed around the islands.

Geography

The main geographical landmass of the Falkland Islands consisted of East Falkland and West Falkland, forming the bulk of the islands' 4,700-square mile (12,000km^2) extent, the rest made up of more than 700 diminutive islands, many of them little more than an acre in area. In distance the islands measure 140 miles (220km) east to west and 87 miles (140km) from north to south, the two landmasses separated by Falkland Sound, a channel roughly 12 miles (20km) in width. Most of the combat operations during the conflict took place on the larger East Falkland, which contained the bulk of the islands' population – including the capital, Stanley. East Falkland was in itself divided on a rough east–west axis by Choiseul Sound and Grantham Sound, the two fjords separated and the two halves joined by a thin isthmus, on which was located Darwin and Goose Green.

The Falklands landscape offered both possibilities and problems for military operations, depending on whether you were in the position of defence or attack. Its coastline was extraordinarily convoluted, with dozens of inlets, bays, anchorages and rough beaches, providing a world of opportunity for amphibious actions. This being said, away from developed harbours such as Port Stanley, Port Fitzroy and Port William, not every bay was well suited to providing anchorage or ship-to-shore access. Indeed, even for small boats the Falklands coastline could be difficult. The mineral-rich waters around the islands, for example, produced very high volumes of kelp. Both Argentine and British Special Forces (SF) and Marines, when attempting to reach the shore in small shallow-draught boats, often found their outboard motors choked into silence by the noose-like kelp, even resorting to oars as the only way to cross the waters.

Quality navigational information around these waters was critical. In this regard, the British were immeasurably assisted by the insight of Major Ewen Southby-Tailyour, RM. As luck would have it, Southby-Tailyour, a talented yachtsman, had been stationed in the Islands from 1978 to 1979, during which he undertook a detailed survey of the Falklands coastline. As he sailed around the coastline, he made copious illustrated notes on its topography and hydrographical details. Major General J.H.A. Thompson (commander of 3 Commando Brigade, Royal Marines, during the Falklands campaign) later remembered how Southby-Tailyour's notes intersected with the war effort: 'On 2 April 1982, when Argentina invaded the Falkland Islands, Ewen presented himself at Hamoaze House in Plymouth, where I had set up my Headquarters, bringing with him the pilotage notebook and a large roll of charts. After a few minutes it was clear that he and his notebook and charts must come south with us – not that he needed any persuading. He became a key member of the team planning the amphibious assault.'[1]

The inland terrain in the Falklands is a mixture of pasture, barren moorland, rocky outcrops and plateaus, and soggy morass, all largely stripped of any lofty vegetation by the cutting South Atlantic winds. The nature

of this terrain would have an inertial effect on infantry operations, particularly on the speed of marching, the likelihood of incidental lower-leg injuries and the bacterial perils of constantly soaked feet.

Although much of the terrain of the Falklands is low-lying, there are key points of elevation around the islands, especially in the northern half of East Falkland, providing a highly defendable landscape on the eastern approaches to Stanley. The highest of these points is to the east, Mount Usbourne at 2,313ft (705m). It should be noted that many of the 'mountains' that would become landmarks in the subsequent fighting were in reality quite geologically modest. Mount Tumbledown, scene of an intense night battle on 13/14 June 1982, was actually just 551ft (168m) high, although this was perfectly elevated enough to provide a defendable position.

The climate also had a signal effect on the parameters of operations in the Falklands. Although the Falkland Islands are on the approaches to Antarctica, the climate is actually in a transitional region between temperate and subarctic zones. What this means in practical terms is that the Falklands are largely moderate in regard to air temperature, with average

summer highs (January being peak summer) of about 13°C (55°F), and average winter lows of -1°C (30°F). While these temperatures might sound perfectly manageable, they are intensified by a combination of very high humidity (which increases heat exchange), frequent driving rain (often turning into a slush snow), thick fogs and immensely strong winds accentuating the wind chill factor. It was a difficult climate in which to operate, threatening the complacent with hypothermia and frostbite. It would therefore test both British and Argentine uniforms, kit and equipment to the maximum. Electrics, batteries and communications were particularly vulnerable to climate damage and atmospheric interference.

The population of the Falklands at the time of the Argentine invasion was about 1,800. The bulk of the inhabitants were concentrated in the capital, Stanley (1,000 people), which was the seat of the island's government, its Executive Committee and Legislative Council led by the Governor, Rex Hunt. The only other significant area of habitation was Goose Green, the remainder of the islanders being largely isolated farming families in scattered settlements, with poor or absent connecting roads. (The lack of adequate roads would have a significant

ABOVE The bays of the Falklands offered the British Task Force several options for amphibious landing sites; the preference was for those with surrounding landscape that partly protected shipping from air and missile attack.
(Defence Picture Library)

SOUTH GEORGIA

Some 810 miles (1,300km) to the south-east of the Falklands, South Georgia became another objective of Argentine invasion in March. This isolated patch of land, 103 miles (165km) long and 1–22 miles (1–35km) wide, had historically been dominated by the whaling industry, but by 1982 this industry had vanished – testified to by several decaying whaling stations along the northern coastline, which provided bases for the British Antarctic Survey (BAS) at King Edward Point and Bird Island. South Georgia's environment is far more extreme than that found on the Falklands. It has a polar climate, with sub-zero temperatures, heavy snowfall and blizzards, freezing rain and thick fogs. The terrain is mountainous, with 11 peaks rising to more than 6,562ft (2,000m), and several of its valleys feature extensive glaciers, the largest of which is the Fortuna Glacier. Although South Georgia is remote in every sense, and had little of economic value to outsiders (albeit possibly as a base for South Atlantic mineral exploitation), like the Falklands it was claimed by the Argentines, on the basis that it was a dependency of those distant islands.

from the Falklands featuring on a British stamp, with exports of just under £5 million.

The ubiquitous sheep provided a means by which British troops, particularly Special Forces (SF) soldiers, could live off the land when on ops far away from the logistical hubs. They could also live off some of the indigenous wildlife, such as rabbits and other rodents, while seals, walruses and penguins are prolific around the islands' coastal regions. The often limited visibility through thick fog on several occasions caused the British and Argentines to launch attacks on what they thought were enemy soldiers, but which turned out to be hapless animals caught in the line of fire.

Preparations for invasion

The basis of the Argentine claim to the Falkland Islands is a complex one, entwined in the colonial machinations of Spain, France and Great Britain from the 16th to the 20th centuries. The exact evolution of the dispute over the islands has been detailed elsewhere. Suffice to say, however, that from 1767, when Louis-Antoine, Comte de Bougainville, transferred the French colony centred on Port Louis to Spanish ownership, the Spanish felt themselves the rightful owners of the islands. This was contested,

effect on the operations, such as keeping the Argentines heavily bottled up around Stanley.) The economy of the island was, and remains, largely based upon sheep farming (sheep were first introduced on to the island in 1835, but numbered more than 600,000 by 1982), fishing and some mineral exploitation, plus an income

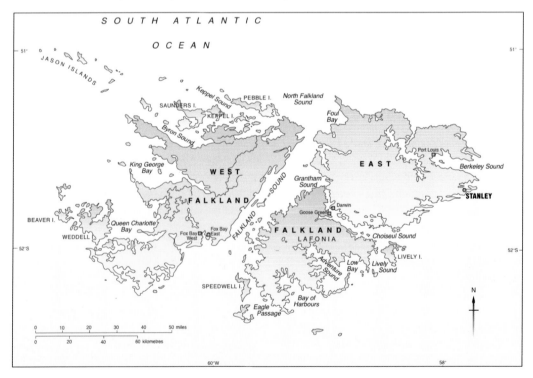

RIGHT A map of the Falklands, showing the two major landmasses (East and West Falkland split by Falkland Sound). The bulk of the Argentine defence was deployed on East Falkland, mostly around Stanley but with a further major outpost at Goose Green and Darwin. *(Defence Picture Library)*

to uncertain degrees by the British, who had established a garrison at Port Egmont, but which it abandoned in 1774; according to Argentine claims, the abandonment had been preceded by a secret commitment to accept Spanish sovereignty.

The Spanish left the islands, which they called the Islas Malvinas, in the early 19th century, and in 1816 Argentina laid its claim to the Falklands. Britain protested this claim, and in 1833 took possession of the islands through military intervention, declaring them a formal British colony in 1842. Tensions over the Falkland Islands thereafter bubbled away for more than a century, but intensified during the second half of the 1970s and into the early 1980s, as the Argentine government looked to divert attention away from domestic political and security issues. In November 1976, Argentina established the illegal Corbeta Uruguay military outpost at Thule in the South Sandwich Islands, 430 miles (700km) south-east of South Georgia, which it retained until 1982 as Britain played through diplomatic responses. Under the Presidency of General Leopoldo Galtieri, who took office in December 1981, the Argentine claims over the Falklands went from aspiration to implementation. Galtieri and his junta had been encouraged by both the perceived weakening of the British forces under the Nott reforms (which would limit the UK's capacity for a long-range expeditionary war), the close alliance that Argentina had built up with the United States and the sense that the British government of Margaret Thatcher was losing interest in the Falklands issue, and might be open to a leasing arrangement with Argentina. Tensions were increased on 20 December 1981, when the Argentine naval icebreaker *Almirante Irízar* entered South Georgian waters without going through the correct international formalities, failing to report to the BAS base commander, Peter Witty.

By January/February 1982, war plans were being developed at the highest levels in Argentina, focused on the invasion of both the Falklands and South Georgia. Key figures in the planning included:

■ Admiral Juan José Lombardo – Chief of Naval Operations
■ Brigadier General Siegfriedo Plessl – Argentine Air Force

ABOVE HMS *Invincible* was under sale to Australia at the outbreak of the Falklands conflict; the war convinced the UK MOD to retain a three-carrier fleet. *(Defence Picture Library)*

BELOW A photograph of the old refrigeration plant at Ajax Bay on East Falkland. Ajax Bay was later to become of one three principal British landing sites around San Carlos Water. *(Defence Picture Library)*

Endurance pictured
off South Georgia
during the operation
to reclaim the island;
HMS *Plymouth*
accompanies her
in the background.
(Defence Picture Library)

■ Major General Osvaldo Garcia – Commander, V Corps
■ Rear Admiral Carlos Büsser – Commander, Argentine Marine Corps
■ Lieutenant Commander Guillermo Santillan – 2-in-C, Argentine Marine Corps
■ Commander Alfredo Weinstabl – Commander, 2nd Marine Infantry Battalion
■ Lieutenant-Commander 'Fatty' Payba – Logistics Officer, 2nd Marine Infantry Battalion.

At this stage, actual operational details had not been sent out to the front-line commanders, but a definite momentum was building. British diplomats and military personnel were reporting signs of Argentine hostility or suspicion, and the possibility of a war in the South Atlantic appears to have filtered through to some parts of the British forces, with increased training in February 1982 in the Brecon Beacons (an environment closely matched to that of the Falklands). A critical incident was the arrival,

on 19 March, of the naval transport vessel ARA *Bahía Buen Suceso* off Leith, South Georgia, again unreported to the governor. Argentine businessman Constantino Davidoff had been contracted by Scottish company, Christian Salvesen, to remove scrap materials from whaling stations around South Georgia, and the *Bahía Buen Suceso* was the ship he chartered to take him there. On board were 41 workers plus a party of Buzo Tactico (the Argentine equivalent of the US Navy SEALs), masquerading as scientists and led by Lieutenant Commander Alfredo Astiz. The vessel anchored off Leith and deployed its personnel without reporting to the authorities. Furthermore, an Argentine flag was planted and a celebratory volley of gunfire was delivered on the beach. Combined with a reconnaissance overflight from an Argentine C-130 aircraft, these events made it clear to Rex Hunt and the British government that Argentina might be about to make more substantial military moves in the South Atlantic. In response, the British diverted the Royal Navy ice patrol vessel HMS *Endurance* under Captain Nick Barker, from the Falklands to South Georgia, complete with its complement of 12 Royal Marines under the command of Lieutenant Keith Mills. Sensing the tensions to the south-east, the RM contingent was further strengthened by nine more Marines from the Falklands garrison.

Endurance arrived off South Georgia on 23 March after a two-day journey. The next day she sailed to Grytviken, the South Georgian capital, where she deployed the Marines, who took over coastal surveillance duties performed by adaptive members of the BAS. For the

HMS *ENDURANCE* – KEY DATA (1982)

Type:	Icebreaker
Displacement:	3,600 long tons (3,658 tonnes)
Length:	305ft (93m)
Beam:	46ft (14m)
Draught:	18ft (5.5m)
Propulsion:	1 × Burmeister & Wain diesel engine
Speed:	14.5 knots (16.7mph or 26.9km/h)
Complement:	119 (including 12 Royal Marines)
Armament:	2 × Oerlikon 20mm cannon
Aircraft carried:	2 × Westland Wasp helicopters

next week, *Endurance* conducted aerial and offshore surveillance, playing a cat-and-mouse game with Argentine counter-responses. The same day, the Argentine naval transport vessel *Bahía Paraiso* sailed into Stromness Bay and deployed 12 naval technicians ashore, including Astiz.

By this time, Argentina was hardening its formal plans to invade the Falkland Islands and South Georgia. Originally the invasion was discussed for September 1982, but the junta decided to move it forward into early April as it became clear that Britain was responding to events and was starting to make military arrangements for a possible conflict. For the junta, it was imperative that action be taken soon, before Britain could deploy defensive forces into the South Atlantic.

British defensive arrangements

The British defence of the Falklands and South Georgia initially rested in the hands of just a few dozen Royal Marines. On the Falklands themselves, there were 69 Marines (officers and men) – 40 Marines of the 1982/83 Detachment of Naval Party 8901, commanded by Major M.J. Norman (who only assumed command on 1 April), and the remnants of the supposedly outgoing 1981/82 Detachment, minus those Marines on South Georgia. There were also a handful of Royal Navy officers, plus the very limited resources of the Falkland Islands Defence Force (FIDF) – a civilian reserve containing a mix of ex-service personnel – although only 27 reported for duty. The barracks for the Marines were situated at the far western end of Stanley Harbour, at Moody Brook.

ABOVE **HMS *Endurance*, the Royal Navy's ice patrol ship, aptly known as the 'Red Plum', 1982. *Endurance* was due to be axed from the fleet on 15 April 1982 as part of defence cuts, but played a central role in the early actions of the Falklands War.** *(Defence Picture Library)*

BELOW **A counterpoint to the Type 42 were the County-class destroyers, distinguished from the former by the twin 4.5in Mk 6 gun on the foredeck.** *(Defence Picture Library)*

but all recognised this was an impossibility. The positions taken by the Marines were as follows:

- Airport – 5 Section
- Yorke Bay Beach – two-man general-purpose machine gun (GPMG) crew
- Hookers Point – 1 Section
- Old airstrip – 2 Section (including Carl Gustaf and 66mm mortar)
- 0.6 miles (1km) further west – 3 Section
- Murrell Heights – 5 Section
- Sapper Hill – two-man observation post (OP)
- Navy Point – 6 Section (with Gemini boat).[2]

Such thinly spread and minor force elements could not hope to make anything other than a token resistance against a major invasion. The fall-back point for all troops was Government House in Stanley.

Over on South Georgia, Keith Mills had very few resources at his disposal in terms of men and weaponry – just 22 Marines, small arms, an 84mm Carl Gustaf recoilless rifle and a number of Light Anti-Armour Weapon (LAW) rockets. Mills distributed his men around King Edward Point, covering the approaches to Grytviken. The best description of their positions comes from Nicholas Van der Bijl, who was an Intelligence Corps officer attached to 3 Cdo Bde during the conflict:

Protected by 100ft scree cliffs, Mills selected a 30ft-high plateau north-west of Shackleton House as his defensive position. As it was still covered in summer tussock grass, concealment was not difficult for the four two-man and two three-man trenches covering the approaches from Grytviken and the King Edward Point beach. Corporal Thomsen's five-strong section and a GPMG were placed in front of Shackleton House to enfilade anyone landing on the beach. A two-man LMG section covered the left flank. The assault engineer Marine Daniels, helped by Marines Porter and Church, mined other

ABOVE Britain had a superb Special Forces community under its command. Here an SAS trooper undergoes an orientation exercise in the UK, in conditions approximating those of the Falklands. *(Defence Picture Library)*

Norman set about implementing a defensive plan, using very limited resources. Recognising that an Argentine invasion would almost certainly focus on the quick capture of Stanley, Port Stanley and the islands' main airfield, Norman divided his men into blocking sections and observation points, and deployed them around Stanley Bay, the intention being to retard Argentine progress towards Stanley itself and prevent the airfield from being captured. The official command was that they hold out for two weeks to allow main British forces to arrive,

LEFT Lieutenant Colonel Nick Vaux chats with his Marines during the Falklands conflict; Vaux served as the commander of 42 Cdo. *(Defence Picture Library)*

beaches below the Customs House and several houses were wired with improvised but lethal explosive devices made from empty ammunition tins and bits of metal. The jetty was mined with a command-detonated 45-gallon oil drum filled with a lethal cocktail of petrol, paint and plastic explosive.[3]

The hope was that Mills' Marines could make a valiant but short defence, enough to spoil the momentum of the Argentine assault, then retreat to the wilderness further north, from where they could mount a guerrilla campaign.

Argentine invasion of the Falklands – Operation Rosario

By late March 1982, the practical arrangements for the invasion of the Falkland Islands had been finalised, and on 28 March the Argentine invasion task force set sail from the Rio del Plata estuary. Invasion forces were separated into three main elements: Task Force 20 (Cover and Support), Task Force 40 (Amphibious) and Task Force 40.1 (Landing Forces). Task Force 20 was essentially a carrier group to provide offshore air and landing support, plus a locus for air traffic control once the airport had been seized. It included the carrier *Veinticinco de Mayo*, five destroyers and a tanker. Task Force 40 included the destroyers *Santísima Trinidad* and *Hercules* (both ex-British Type 42 destroyers), the frigates *Drummond* and *Granville* and the Balao-class submarine *Santa Fe*, transporting a force of tactical divers. The actual invasion would be carried out by Task Force 40.1, the key elements of which were the vessels *Cabo San Antonio* and *Almirante Irízar*, carrying the landing force of 874 men, composed from the following units:

- A Company, 1st Marine Infantry Battalion
- D and E Companies, 2nd Marine Infantry Battalion
- 1st Platoon, C Company, 25th Infantry Regiment
- Amphibious Commando Grouping (Buzo Tactico troops)

- 1st Amphibious Vehicle Company (LTVP-7 and LARC-5 amphibious armoured vehicles)
- Support elements: 1 × 105mm rocket battery (Marine); 1 × anti-aircraft battery (Marine); combat engineers.

As finalised on 1 April 1982, the invasion plan was as follows. The Buzo Tactico was to have a leading role, being deployed at Mullet Creek south of Stanley, then advancing north to capture the Moody Brook barracks and Government House. Support for the commandos would be provided, as required, by the men of the 2nd Marines. Meanwhile, the platoon of men from the 25th Infantry Regiment were to move quickly and seize the airport (originally it was intended to send them out to capture Goose Green); once the airport was in Argentine hands, reinforcements from the 25th Infantry could be flown in.

It should be noted that while popular history has presented the Argentine soldiers as ill-trained conscripts – indeed many of the subsequent forces deployed to the islands were just that – the men going ashore for what was called Operation Rosario were of excellent quality, being well-trained, disciplined and highly motivated.

The invasion of the Falkland Islands began on 2 April 1982. Ninety-two men of the Amphibious Commando Grouping were deployed under cover of darkness from the *Santísima Trinidad* on 1 April using Gemini

BELOW Looking somewhat cold and apprehensive, Argentine troops come ashore during Operation Rosario on 2 April 1982. *(Defence Picture Library)*

ABOVE Port Stanley: the main settlement and the capital of the Falkland Islands, with a population of about 1,000 people. *(Andy Cole)*

boats, commanded by Lieutenant Commander Guillermo Sanchez-Sabarots. They had a tortuous journey in the small boats buffeted by rough seas and often stopped by the near-impenetrable kelp beds, but they eventually made it ashore, later meeting up with other commandos from the *Santa Fe*. After a five-hour advance, they approached Moody Brook around 05:30hrs and made an assault,

BELOW A Royal Navy Oberon-class submarine. Although this diesel-electric submarine type did not have the underwater endurance of its nuclear-powered counterparts, they were useful for littoral warfare amphibious deployments. *(Defence Picture Library)*

using grenades and small arms. It was at this point that they discovered that Moody Brook was actually entirely abandoned. Meanwhile, another team of commandos, led by Lieutenant Commander Pedro Giachino, was moving in on Government House. Here the Falklands became a true shooting war. Giachino and another commando were shot and wounded by two RMs as the Argentines attempted to move into Government House. Giachino would later die of his wounds. Three other Argentine soldiers were forced to hide in the maid's loft. A firefight now developed around the building.

The sounds of gunfire alerted Norman to the action around Government House, and also to the realisation that his troops were facing in the wrong direction. He therefore radioed all his troops and instructed them to pull back to Government House, to concentrate his force. But now the full-scale invasion was launched against the British. The *Cabo San Antonio*, escorted by *Drummond*, a corvette, and the destroyer *Hercules* at 06:20hrs disembarked the marines and infantry aboard more than 20 amtracs, which headed into the waters of Yorke Bay. On one of the vessels was Rear Admiral Carlos Büsser. At 06:45hrs further troops were landed by helicopter on to the airfield, where E Company LTVP-7s and troops of the 25th Infantry had already secured the airfield against no opposition. The column of amtracs moving towards Stanley were not so fortunate. Near the Ionospheric Research Station the RMs had established some improvised roadblocks, and when the amtracs slowed they were hit with machine-gun, 66mm LAW (light anti-tank weapon) and Carl Gustaf fire, the latter disabling one vehicle.

Despite such aggressive actions, the inevitable outcome of the day's action was drawing to a close. Stanley was occupied and Government House was surrounded. Those Marines who didn't make it to Government House were scattered from their positions. More and more Argentine reinforcements were pouring into the islands. Shortly after daybreak, the Marines and the government of the Falklands made a formal surrender, to spare unnecessary loss of life. The Marines had only been able to resist for a day, rather than two weeks, but given the scale of the forces they faced, nothing greater could truly be expected of them.

Argentine invasion of South Georgia – Operation Paraquet

The action on South Georgia on 3 April 1982 was a minor one in the overall sweep of British history, but it has gone down as a remarkable example of British military tenacity. At 10:30hrs, into Stromness Bay sailed the Argentine frigate *Guerrico* and the *Bahía Paraíso*, the latter containing a force of some 100 marines (they had been transferred from the *Guerrico*). The frigate, a French A69 type, was of particular concern for the British, principally on account of her 100mm/55 Mod. 1968 dual-purpose gun on the forecastle, 40mm Bofors L/70 anti-aircraft gun and two 20mm Oerlikons, all of which could be depressed to fire at ground and coastal land targets. The *Bahía Paraíso* also brought onboard Puma and Alouette helicopters; the former conducted a recce of the landing areas, while the Puma began transferring marines ashore.

If the Argentines had expected that the display of force would compel an instant surrender, they would be disappointed. Just after midday, both the *Bahía Paraíso*, commanded by Captain C. Trombetta, and then the *Guerrico* (Captain Alfonso), moved into Cumberland East Bay, the frigate aiming its guns at Shackleton House in a clear threat. The Puma was now making its second relay to shore, with 15 marines aboard, but as he approached the landing point on the beach – with the Alouette also nearby – the RMs opened up on the helicopters with heavy automatic fire. Two of the Argentine marines were killed in the fusillade, and the Puma limped off to crash-land on the shore opposite King Edward Point. The Alouette was also slightly damaged.

But more shocking British resistance was to come. The Marines began to engage the Argentine troops as they advanced toward Shackleton House. This brought a counterfire response from *Guerrico*, which opened up with its 100mm gun. Mills therefore ordered his Marines on the coast to engage the frigate with everything they had; the confines of King Edward Cove meant that the ship lost much of its manoeuvrability, and at 600yd (550m) distance

Phoenix Assurance Bicentenary

SUD ATLANTICA

Founded 1876
108th Year — 2005 (new series)

Buenos Aires Herald

EL HERALDO DE BUENOS AIRES

1782–1982

BUENOS AIRES, SATURDAY, APRIL 3, 1982

16 Pages · Price: $ 5.000.-
Air mail $ 100.- surcharge

Thatcher pressured to fight

Argentina recovers Malvinas by force

ARGENTINA yesterday unilaterally put an end to a century and a half of vain negotiations to establish its right to govern the Malvinas islands by sending in a 4,000-man invasion force to take them over from their British administrators.

The pre-dawn landing included members of the three Argentine armed forces who easily overcame the handful of British troops stationed at Port Stanley, the Malvinas capital.

There was, however, armed resistance to the occupation, in which one Argentine officer died and another officer and an enlisted man were injured.

The Argentine Navy High Command reported yesterday afternoon that during the landing of the first wave of Argentine Marines, there was a firefight

• A group of soldiers raise the Argentine flag at dawn yesterday on the Malvinas islands. (DYN photo supplied by the Argentine Navy)

with the British Royal Marines. During the fighting, Captain Pedro Giachino, "who advanced heroically at the head of his men" on the British positions, was shot dead. Wounded were Navy Lieutenant Diego Garcia Quiroga and Petty Officer Ernesto Urbina.

The operation was termed a complete success by the Argentine military who announced that the islands with their 1,900 inhabitants were under complete Argentine control following the surrender of British Governor Rex Hunt, who was earlier reported to have ordered the Royal Marines to cease resistance.

Argentine naval sources indicated last night that military protocol had been observed to the utmost, with the British personnel and island residents being treated with total consideration by the occupation force. The sources said that orders were also strict for the treatment of the British flag which was reportedly granted upon its removal the same respect given the Argentine colours which were run up.

On securing the islands the junta put out a communiqué in which it stated that "a long period of fruitless negotiations has come to an end" and added that the "Argentine people ...feel the happiness of having obtained just recourse on their demands for (recuperation of) their legitimate rights."

The communiqué then went on to say that the junta, "as the supreme organ of state, informs the people of the Argentine nation that today the republic, through the armed forces, (which) carried out a successful joint operation, has regained the Malvinas, the South Georgia and Sandwich islands for the national patrimony."

The junta later in the day announced that it was ordering the evacuation of British military

and administrative personnel which had been serving in the Malvinas. These people were expected to be flown to a British diplomatic mission elsewhere in Latin America. The Argentine Air Force would, the junta indicated, take care of the evacuation, shipping the British subjects out of Comodoro Rivadavia.

In London, British Prime Minister Margaret Thatcher called an emergency session of her cabinet as the British Royal Navy began feverish work to muster a naval task force to send to the south Atlantic, but last night at press time, she had apparently still not taken a definite decision as to whether or not to fight to regain control of the islands.

Sources in London made it clear that some British ships were already on their way to the islands while London worked at preparing a bigger more powerful strike force.

Meanwhile Mrs Thatcher faced a political storm which was brewing in parliament as the morning newspapers were last night preparing editions which would call on her to make the decision to go to war to wrest the islands from Argentine control.

The right-wing Daily Express published a frontpage photo of a group of islanders with the caption: "Our loyal subjects—we must defend them".

The Sun, a conservative tabloid, said simply, "It's war!" in an exclamation which covered most of the front page.

The Daily Mail opted for "Shamed!" as its main headline, while The Times, the voice of the British establishment, urged that further efforts to resolve the conflict by diplomacy should be made "only as a prelude to taking action".

The Times added: "We still have one of the world's most powerful navies, including a number of nuclear-powered submarines, one at least of which is almost certainly now close to the scene."

President Galtieri and the military junta made it clear in their statements yesterday after the successful occupation of the Malvinas that Argentina would answer with force any attempt by the British at a counterattack to retake the islands. (UP, Reuters, NA, DYN, and own sources).

Britain demands immediate withdrawal from islands

United Nations

BRITAIN asked the UN Security Council yesterday to demand the immediate withdrawal of all Argentine forces from the Malvinas islands following what it called a massive invasion.

Submitting a resolution and appealing for its unanimous adoption, Sir Anthony Parsons, Britain's chief delegate, said: "I cannot find words strong enough to express my government's condemnation of this wanton act of armed force."

The Argentine delegate, Eduardo Roca, replied that his government has recovered for its national sovereignty the Malvinas which Britain had wained since 1833.

He said there were no civilian casualties in the Argentine military action that ended "a situation of tension and injustice."

Argentina was prepared to negotiate its differences with Britain, but sovereignty over the Malvinas, off South America, was not negotiable, he said.

The 15-nation Security Council deferred a scheduled debate on Nicaraguan charges against the

United States to take up the Malvinas crisis.

After hearing the British and Argentine statements, members adjourned. They were expected to meet later yesterday to consider the British resolution.

The resolution would have the Security Council demand an immediate cessation of hostilities, demand the immediate withdrawal of all Argentine forces and call on the Argentine and British governments to seek a diplomatic solution and respect the purposes and principles of the UN charter.

Through a statement by its president, the Security Council on Thursday night called on both sides to observe the utmost restraint and refrain from the use

or threat of force.

Sir Anthony accepted that appeal, but Roca did not respond.

When the Security Council met yesterday Sir Anthony said Argentina had ignored the appeal by the council president, Kamanda Wa Kamanda of Zaire, and two appeals by UN Secretary General Javier Perez de Cuellar.

Sir Anthony yesterday called the Argentine action a blatant violation of the UN charter and of international law.

"It is an attempt to impose by force a foreign and unwanted control over 1,900 peaceful agricultural people who have chosen in free and fair elections to maintain their links with Britain and the British way of life," he said. (Reuters)

Thousands gather at plaza

PRESIDENT Leopoldo Galtieri, spoke to a crowd of about 10,000 people gathered yesterday afternoon opposite Government House in the historic Plaza de Mayo square.

He received an enthusiastic ovation as he appeared on one of

the balconies of the Casa Rosada and spoke for several minutes.

The President's improvised speech was interrupted several times as the crowd clapped and cheered as he announced the country's recovery of the disputed islands.

Galtieri said his government and the Argentine people would accept talks with the British government following Argentina's forcible takeover of the islands, but "dignity and national pride will be maintained at all costs."

(Continued on page 7)

Vieja Lavanda Fulton
Jabón - Espuma de Afeitar - After Loción - After Crema - Loción - Desodorante

---

from the shore it was within the range of the Marines' rifles, machine guns, LAWs and the Carl Gustaf. The British fire was blistering, and took the *Guerrico* by surprise. The 7.62mm bullets rippled across the length of the ship, and RM David Coombes, operating the Carl Gustaf, even managed to hole the ship below the waterline with his first shot, killing one sailor and causing the sudden ingress of seawater. RM Sergeant Leach, lying on a table in Shackleton House, fired at the bridge of the ship with his sniper rifle, sending the officers diving to the floor.

Incredibly, the *Guerrico*, once-confident in its stature, was now compelled to turn and run, pursued all the way by small-arms fire and rockets from the Carl Gustaf and LAWs. Yet steadily, the tide was turning against the British. One Marine, Corporal Peters, had been seriously wounded by fire from the frigate and, despite

ABOVE The *Buenos Aires Herald* proudly proclaims the invasion and occupation of the Falkland Islands, in its words putting to an 'end a century and a half of vain negotiations'. *(Defence Picture Library)*

ABOVE An aerial photograph of the Goose Green area, defended principally by the Argentine 12th Infantry Regiment. *(Defence Picture Library)*

the threat, Argentine helicopters had been able to build up an appreciable force of their own marines on the coastline. One group of marines, led by 2nd Lieutenant Luna, had moved up to Grytviken, threatening to swing behind the RM positions. So it was that Mills made a judicious decision, having made a very clear statement to the Argentines, and surrendered his force.

Argentine defensive arrangements

To jubilation back home, Argentina had now taken the Falkland Islands and South Georgia, albeit not quite as convincingly as they might have wished for, given the superiority in invasion forces. But it almost immediately became apparent that the intended Argentine strategy for retaining the conquests – using

RIGHT Argentine soldiers in defensive positions on the Falklands with their FN FAL rifles, armed almost identically to the British troops facing them. *(Defence Picture Library)*

international diplomacy and British inertia – was not going to play out, as Britain was now very visibly marshalling a military task force. Argentina might have to make a military defence of the Falklands against one of the world's most experienced and professional armies.

It was now critical that Argentina reinforce the islands heavily, and prepare defensive positions. This was conducted under a new command structure, designated the Malvinas Joint Command (MJC), which in turn was part of the *Teatro de Operaciones del Atlántico Sur* (TOAS, South Atlantic Theatre of Operations), headed by Vice Admiral Juan José Lombardo. In overall charge as commander of the MJC and as the new military governor of the islands was Brigadier General Mario Benjamin Menéndez. His effective 2-in-C, and the Chief of Staff (Operations) was General Américo Daher of the 9th Infantry Brigade, General Oscar Joffre, commander of the 10th Infantry Brigade and of the Puerto Argentina Group of Forces, and finally General Omar Parada, commander of the 3rd Infantry Brigade and of the Malvinas Group of Forces. As events would prove, the command relationship between these four men was to be fractious and unclear. Arguments between the commanders and a distinct lack of inter-service cooperation are two main ingredients in the recipe of Argentine failure on the Falklands.

At the time of the invasion, Argentine forces numbered just 2,000 men. As the British military response became apparent, therefore, it was evident that these numbers would have to increase dramatically. The military could draw on some high-quality troops, especially the marines and some infantry formations, such as the 25th Infantry Regiment, but it was clear that it would also have to draw upon large volumes of conscripts. Conscripts actually composed about 75% of all Argentine soldiers. In both the Army and the Marine Corps, new conscripts were generally channelled into the 3rd Company, while recruits with more training and experience under their belts went into the 2nd Company. Therefore, even with a strong 1st Company and the generally decent quality of NCOs, most formations in no way reached the standards of the regular British forces. In the Falklands conflict, the situation was doubly compounded by the fact that the

new wave of conscripts, *Soldado Clase 63* (*ie* born in 1962), had only joined the ranks a few months previously, and were therefore woefully unprepared for a complex land war. Reserves from the *Soldado Clase 62* were also drawn in, but still the readiness remained poor. It is evident that Argentina's decision to invade in April 1982 – not September as had originally been mooted – was to have significant and sometimes mortal consequences in terms of preparedness.

The influx of men drew the island's garrison up to a force of more than 12,000 men, principally of the 10th Motorised Infantry Brigade, the 3rd Mechanised Infantry Brigade, the 25th Infantry Regiment and the 5th Marine Infantry Battalion, plus numerous supporting units. After much rearrangement, the disposition of forces on the islands are shown in the table below.

Even allowing for the unpreparedness of significant numbers of the Argentine soldiers, this was still a formidable force for the British, especially as the Argentines were generally well equipped and had the benefit of proximate supply centres on the mainland. Yet the forces steaming towards them from across the Atlantic were the greatest the British armed services had mustered since Korea.

Position	Formations/units	Total strength at position
Stanley (town, approaches and airfield)	10th Motorised Infantry Brigade reinforced with: 3rd Infantry Regiment 4th Infantry Regiment 6th Infantry Regiment 7th Infantry Regiment 5th Marine Battalion 25th Infantry Regiment 3rd Artillery Battalion 181st Armoured Cavalry Squadron 181st Military Police and Intelligence Company 601st Anti-Aircraft Battalion (-)*	8,400
Goose Green	From 3rd Brigade: 12th Infantry Regiment 601st Anti-Aircraft Battalion (-) Half-battery of 105mm guns (3 pieces)	1,200
Fox Bay	From 3rd Brigade: 8th Motorised Infantry Regiment (-) 9th Engineer Company (-)	889
Port Howard	From 3rd Brigade: 5th Infantry Regiment 9th Engineer Company (-)	788
Pebble Island	Naval Air Units	120

*Note: (-) – indicates a reduced-strength unit with detached elements

Chapter Two

Task Force logistics and deployment

The British Task Force put together for the reconquest of the Falkland Islands was a triumph not so much of planning, but of willpower and improvisation. In a matter of days, with little forewarning, all elements of the armed services pulled together into a huge military formation, with heavy support from civilian maritime agencies and personnel. It was emphatically a force intended for war, not for diplomacy. Logistically, it also constituted one of the greatest achievements of the post-1945 British military.

OPPOSITE RFA *Stromness*, HMS *Fearless*, RFA *Tidespring* and HMS *Achilles* sailed parallel to one another to perform a replenishment-at-sea operation as the Task Force sailed south. *(Defence Picture Library)*

Argentina would be startled by the rapidity with which the British rose to the challenge of the Falklands invasion, both diplomatically and militarily. Diplomatically, the key result was to bring about the unequivocal condemnation of the invasion by the UN Security Council on 2 April, an outcome Argentina had not been expecting. On that same day, Prime Minister Margaret Thatcher delivered a career-defining speech in the House of Commons, in which she made explicit what was to occur.

The Government have now decided that a large task force will sail as soon as all preparations are complete. HMS Invincible *will be in the lead and will leave port on Monday. [...] The people of the Falkland Islands, like the people of the United Kingdom, are an island race. Their way of life is British; their allegiance is to the Crown. They are few in number, but they have the right to live in peace, to choose their own way of life and to determine their own allegiance. It is the wish of the British people and the duty of Her Majesty's Government to do everything that we can to uphold that right. That will be our hope and our endeavour and, I believe, the resolve of every Member of the House.* [1]

Although Mrs Thatcher's speech declared future intent, in fact practical preparations and even deployments had already been under way for several days.

Assembling the Task Force

Preparations for, or at least discussion about, the possibility of sending a Task Force into the South Atlantic actually began within the British government before Argentine boots touched the ground in the Falklands. By 27 March, it became clear that an invasion was likely, and that it was imperative to deploy assets and reinforcements as soon as possible. Pre-invasion deployments were the RFA ship *Fort Austin*, intended to supply HMS *Endurance* (which had now been ordered to stay around the Falklands), and two RN nuclear-powered submarines, *Spartan* and *Splendid*; both

sailed on 1 April, with *Conqueror* following on 4 April. The decision to deploy no fewer than three submarines was striking in its ambition, and was greeted with some protestations on account of the significant draw on limited global resources (the Cold War was still on, after all). Yet the deployment also placed a threatening but unseen limitation on Argentine naval movements around the Falklands, once the assets arrived there some three weeks after having set sail.

The firm decision to send a major Task Force to the Falklands came on 31 March, much to the credit of arguments presented by Admiral Sir Henry Leach, First Sea Lord, to the Prime Minister, John Nott and a group of other political and military heavyweights. Although the required scale, speed and distance of any deployment initially seemed to argue against the possibility of a war in the South Atlantic, Leach

convinced the Prime Minister and others that it was in fact doable, and that ships, personnel and equipment could be assembled and start sailing within days. Thus Operation Corporate – the British military operation to retake the Falklands Islands – was born.

The assembly of a Task Force was a truly daunting task. It revolved around the following key priorities:

1) Assemble and deploy ground forces sufficient to engage and defeat numerically superior Argentine forces on the Falklands in a land campaign.
2) Assemble and deploy warships sufficient to provide protection for the Task Force against Argentine surface and underwater naval threats, establishing an MEZ around the islands.
3) Assemble and deploy sufficient air assets to provide both battlefield logistical support (rotary

aircraft), CAS and, most important, Combat Air Patrol (CAP) against Argentine air attacks.
4) Assemble and deploy sufficient shipping to transport and manage the logistics to support all of the above, and physically to transport personnel to theatre.
5) Assemble and deploy all requisite amphibious assets to make a combat landing on the Falklands coastline.
6) Establish a means of aerial and maritime resupply for the distant Task Force, which could be maintained throughout the campaign.

The Herculean effort of achieving all of the above would be accomplished by some 30,000 individuals. Two men took the ultimate share of command responsibility, however. The overall commander of the Falklands operation was Admiral Sir John Fieldhouse, Commander-in-Chief Fleet. Although he would not be present

ABOVE The scene at Devonport in 1982, as vessels are prepared for Task Force deployment. The civilian workforce supported the military efforts with a 24/7 cycle of work. Leander-class frigate HMS *Minerva* is on the left. *(Defence Picture Library)*

in theatre, he directed operations via satellite communications from the Fleet Operations Room in Northwood, North London. He would be assisted by the following individuals on his command staff:

- Major General J.J. Moore – Land Forces Deputy (later succeeded by Lieutenant General Sir Richard Trant)
- Air Marshal Sir John Curtiss – Air Commander
- Vice Admiral P.G.M. Herbert – Flag Officer Submarines.

In terms of in-theatre commanders, the overall commander of the Task Force was Rear Admiral J.F. 'Sandy' Woodward, then serving as Flag Officer 1st Flotilla. For the campaign, his operational commanders included:

- Commodore M.C. Clapp – Amphibious Task Group
- Brigadier J.H. Thompson, RM – Landing Force Task Group and 3 Commando Brigade RM
- Major-General Moore RM – Land Forces Falklands Islands
- Brigadier M.J.A. Wilson – 5th Infantry Brigade.

BELOW **Royal Marines accommodated in the carrier HMS** *Hermes* **on the way south; note the Sea King helicopters in the hangar deck at the rear.** *(Defence Picture Library)*

Land forces

The Royal Marines were a first choice for a lead formation in the Falklands land campaign, and indeed would remain a dominant force and command structure throughout. A true elite in the British armed services, the Marines were superbly trained (basic training for enlisted men alone was a punishing 32 weeks) and specialists in amphibious warfare, which would be critical for the Falklands deployment. The command formation was 3 Commando Brigade RM, which contained three battalion-sized (c650 men) units: 40, 42 and 45 Commandos (Cdos). A further advantage of the RM was its self-contained nature. Whatever units deployed to the Falklands had to be capable of considerable independence, and the Marines were developed for just such self-sustaining actions. In addition to its main Cdos, it could also take with it 105mm artillery support with 29 Commando Artillery, RA (Army, but Commando trained), an air squadron (of 18 helicopters at Yeovilton, 9 Gazelle and 6 Scout helicopters would go to the Falklands), a Blowpipe air defence troop, the 1st Raiding Squadron for light coastal assault and surveillance, 59 Commando Squadron Royal Engineers (RE) and the Commando Logistics Regiment – the latter would take the lion's share of logistical responsibility for all ground forces, not just the Marines, during the campaign. A further bonus of 3 Commando was that since 1970 it had conducted Arctic warfare training in Norway; the skills of Arctic operations and survival would be invaluable in the context of the Falklands.

Orders to mobilise 3 Commando came through early on 2 April. Simply gathering the widely dispersed men was a challenge – many Marines were on Eastern leave, and the Cdos were widely scattered around the UK and further afield – 45 Cdo was in Brunei. Nevertheless, with improvisation and energy the RM forces were assembled; they would be shipped down to the Falklands on *Canberra*, *Elk*, *Europic Ferry* and *Norland*.

SF were also to play a major role in the Falklands War. D and G Squadrons of 22 Special Air Service (SAS) Regiment and units of the Special Boat Service (SBS) were deployed, used for both raiding actions and crucial surveillance ops; in many cases, the SAS and SBS were the only sources of intelligence about Argentine land forces. One of the advantages of the SBS, apart from their elite skills in infantry and amphibious warfare, was their close operational alliance with the Royal Marines, having conducted Arctic and Mountain Warfare training with 3 Cdo Bde.

From 3 April, British Army units were also added to force strength. The Parachute Regiment contributed the 2nd and 3rd Battalions (2 Para and 3 Para); 3 Para was the first to mobilise, and sailed with Marines on 9 April on SS *Canberra*, while 2 Para was given five days' notice to move, and left on 26 April on MV *Norland*. The Paras were the other elite element of the 'Red and Green machine' (referring to the respective beret colours of the Paras and the Marines), and although there was a mutual respect between the two formations, the competitive desire to outperform the other could be usefully channelled in active service.

Other Army elements added in support included the following:

- B Squadron, Blues & Royals – 4 × Scorpion, 4 × Scimitar armoured vehicles
- T Battery, 12 Air Defence Regiment – 12 × Rapiers
- 666 Army Air Corps Squadron – 3 × Scout AH.1 helicopters
- 29 Battery, 4 Field Regiment, RA – 6 × 105mm Light Guns (attached to 2 Para).

ABOVE Marine Andy Cole (centre) poses with other men of the Commando Logistics Regiment, the principal combat logistic force for the entire campaign. *(Defence Picture Library)*

LEFT Living conditions aboard the ships destined for the Falklands could be spartan to say the least, especially as many vessels were filled beyond intended capacity. *(Defence Picture Library)*

Numerous other smaller elements found themselves quickly mobilised and deployed for operations, including troops from 43 Air Defence Battery; 32 Guided Weapons Regiment, Royal Artillery (RA); 16 Field Ambulance Corps, Royal Army Medical Corps (RAMC); and 49 Explosive Ordnance Disposal (EOD) Squadron, Royal Engineers (RE).

Together these forces presented some of the best and most capable units within the British armed services, but there remained the nagging concern that the troop strength did not meet the requirements to achieve dominance over a well-prepared enemy in defensive positions. On 25 April, therefore, it was decided to reinforce with a further brigade of infantry. The 5th Infantry Brigade was chosen; it was specifically designated as an 'out-of-NATO area' formation, which meant that it could be deployed without unsettling the Army's NATO commitments in Europe. Nevertheless, two of the brigade's key units – 2 and 3 Para – had already been sent south, hence they had to be replaced. For this 5 Inf Bde turned to two Guards battalions – the 1st Welsh and 2nd Scots – both of which had been largely performing ceremonial duties. Recognising that they needed some preparation for deployment, both Guards units quickly headed out to the Sennybridge training area

in the Brecon Beacons, Wales, where they could acclimatise to operational conditions approaching those in the Falklands. The other key infantry unit, integral to 5 Inf Bde, was the 1st/7th Gurkha Rifles. In total this large battalion (it contained four rifle companies instead of the typical three) added 720 men to the mix. Like 3 Cdo Bde, 5 Inf Bde would also bring a broad mix of artillery, air defence, engineer, aviation, comms/signals, medical, EOD and administrative support units, the final contribution being 3,200 men, giving a total land force of some 10,500 troops.

Logistical challenges

Overcoming the logistical demands of pulling together all the supplies and materiel for this large force, and transferring them from numerous depots to the supply ships, was little short of miraculous. There were three central problems:

1) Sourcing all supplies quickly from scattered depots and storage points;
2) Transporting them quickly to the ports (and sourcing enough vehicles to do so);
3) Loading them into the ships for departure.

The full story of the logistical preparations of the Task Force is a complex one, replete with amazing stories of ingenuity at small-group level. (For example, on HMS *Invincible*, 30 men were tasked with sourcing and delivering 180,000 eggs in just 20 hours.) What was distinctive about this phase, however, was how the genuine threat of war mobilised both inter-service and military–civilian cooperation with heartening practicality and goodwill, often waving aside the peacetime paperwork and bureaucratic banalities.

For supplying the ground forces, the logistical burden fell heavily upon the Commando Logistics Regiment, formed in 1971–72. Although the regiment was ostensibly dedicated to supporting 3 Cdo Bde, in reality it often provided joint services support, and for the Falklands preparation it was utterly integral. Its responsibilities increased commensurately with the addition of Parachute Regiment troops to the mix, responsibilities that it had to handle

BELOW Emotional farewells as the Task Force sets sail. The Falklands War ignited a sense of patriotism in large parts of the British public – emotions that hadn't been so openly displayed since the Second World War. *(Defence Picture Library)*

without an increase in manpower. The key leadership figure in Commando logistics for the Falklands was Colonel Ian Baxter of the Royal Corps of Transport, and Deputy Chief of Staff to Major General Jeremy Moore. Baxter and his staff created a whirlwind of activity within hours of the command to move. They drew on the resources of the UKLF G3 Transport and Movement Branch, as well as the brigade's own transportation assets, and started collecting and moving thousands of 1-ton pallets of war reserve supplies from depots around the country, the first shipments beginning just 25 minutes after initial orders.

The scale of what followed is perfectly summed up in this passage from *Logistics in the Falklands War: A Case Study in Expeditionary Warfare* by Kenneth L. Privratsky, recommended reading for anyone wanting to understand the logistics of the campaign in full detail:

> Mileage travelled during these first days by trucks from the Commando Logistics Regiment alone equated to driving to the Falkland Islands and back seven times. UKLF eventually utilized 1,500 trucks of various sizes to meet the demands for movement, including over 100 vehicles hired from commercial carriers. Containers played no role in the movement of supplies. All cargo moved either on pallets or loose in packs, what is commonly referred to as break-bulk; and a lot of smaller packages moved hand-over-hand up ramps, down corridors and into storage areas. Supply

ABOVE Gurkha troops keep in shape during the passage through the South Atlantic by going for a run around the deck of the *QE2*.
(Defence Picture Library)

LEFT Troops conduct deck PT aboard SS *Canberra*. Note the Wombat anti-tank weapons in the foreground; these were not actually deployed in action.
(Defence Picture Library)

depots dispatched a million operational ration packs and twelve million normal meals; nearly 10,000 tons of ammunition; 1,260 tons of POL; and 3,880 tons of ordnance stores. A large part of all of it was loaded within seventy-two hours. Before the full deployment was over, a whopping 38,000 tons would move from depots throughout the United Kingdom to ships for loading.[3]

One important point to note is that in the assembling of the Task Force the priority at first was simply to get the supplies on to ships, and get the ships under way. There was no tactical combat loading at this stage, beyond that already built into some stocks. Almost all of the combat loading would be performed at sea, internally aboard each ship and also through almost continuous cross-decking (the swapping or transfer of resources between ships, typically performed by helicopters).

Maritime logistics

The Royal Navy was also engaged in the greatest logistical challenge it had faced since the Second World War. Not only did it have to assemble a warfighting fleet (covered in depth in Chapter 3), but it also had to oversee the sourcing, refitting and defence of a huge number of civilian vessels, requisitioned for war purposes and to plug the gaps in fleet capability.

For a start, there was the issue of dockyard facilities, both for loading supplies and for performing the many ship conversions required (see below). The initial hope was that much of the work could be done at regular commercial ports. It soon became clear, however, that practicalities such as security, facilities available, labour skills and also restrictions on handling sensitive loads (such as ammunition), meant that most of these locations were not suited to the operation. Thus the burden fell upon the Marchwood Military Port at Southampton and the Royal Navy Dockyards at Portsmouth, Devonport, Chatham, Portland, Rosyth and Gibraltar.

The Falklands War came at a very sensitive time for British military dockyards. Chatham and Gibraltar had already been mooted for closure, and on the very day of the Argentine invasion, redundancy notices had been issued to large numbers of dockyard workers at Portsmouth. Yet at a time when many workers could have made political capital out of the situation, instead they laboured tirelessly to ensure that the British Task Force went off to war at proper strength. Dockyard facilities also required much rapid redevelopment to cope with both the volume of supplies being shifted and also the scale of ship refitting involved. As an example of the scale of work, Portsmouth alone performed 7 major ship conversions and 14 minor conversions, all in a matter of days.

The logistical backbone of the Royal Navy was the RFA, and for the Falklands it committed nearly its entire strength – 22 out of 27 vessels. Fleet Replenishment Ships were responsible for carrying and providing ammunition, food and dry stores. To perform cross-decking, the ships used either jackstays rigged between vessels, or their onboard Wessex or Sea King helicopters. Next were the large Fleet Tankers, which carried furnace fuel oil (required by some of the older vessels in the fleet, such as *Hermes*), diesel fuel and aviation fuel, and also fresh water. There were also Support Tankers, which served to keep the Fleet Tankers' holds

BELOW The Landing Ship Logistic (LSL) RFA *Sir Bedivere* (L3004) in the foreground, with another LSL in the background. The Sir Lancelot class of vessels had a troop-carrying capacity of more than 400 men, and could deploy multiple vehicles, up to Main Battle Tank (MBT) size. *(Defence Picture Library)*

RIGHT The two Fearless-class Landing Platform Dock (LPD) vessels could deploy between 400 and 700 troops on amphibious operations, via four LCUs in the stern dock and four smaller landing craft from davits. *(Defence Picture Library)*

full, but could also refuel other ships directly. Fuel and water replenishment at sea was done by hose, the larger Fleet Tankers being able to refuel three ships at once. Water was also a significant issue for the Task Fleet, as although many of the RN ships had reverse osmosis systems for producing potable water, many of the civilian ships did not; the RN water-making facilities also often couldn't cope with the capacity demands, their decks crowded with extra personnel. Hence the need for tankers.

A type of RFA ship particularly critical to Operation Corporate – the operation to recover the Falklands – were the Landing Ship Logistics (LSLs), large amphibious seagoing vessels that featured both bow and stern doors for loading and unloading supplies and vehicles. Six of these ships would ultimately make the journey south: *Sir Bedivere*, *Sir Galahad*, *Sir Geraint*, *Sir Lancelot*, *Sir Percivale* and *Sir Tristram*.

Yet as much as the RFA could take on its share of the logistical burden, the viability of the entire Task Force to a large extent hung upon an armada of Ships Taken Up From Trade (STUFT), civilian vessels that could, under government emergency powers, be requisitioned for national service. The debt to these vessels is succinctly summed up in the aptly titled *They Couldn't Have Done It Without Us* by John Johnson-Allen, a detailed history of the contribution of the merchant navy to the Falklands campaign:

> To support the Royal Navy in the Falklands War, 52 ships from 33 different companies were taken over by the government. In addition, 22 Royal Fleet Auxiliary (RFA) ships crewed by Merchant Navy personnel, were in support. The roles that were undertaken included troopships, hospital ships, minesweepers, support ships, dispatch ships and tugs. Approximately 70 per cent of all the ships involved in the Falklands War were manned by the Merchant Navy.[4]

LEFT A Wessex helicopter performs a Resupply at Sea (RAS). In one day alone, Wessex helicopters flew 138 RAS sorties from Ascension Island. *(Defence Picture Library)*

These figures underline the logistical backbone the merchant navy provided for the Task Force. One is struck by the diversity of the vessels brought into war service. At the more majestic end of the spectrum were the big luxury cruise liners, specifically the *Canberra* (for transporting 3 Cdo Bde troops) and the *Queen Elizabeth 2* (5 Inf Bde). The SS *Uganda*, a smaller cruise ship, was repurposed as a hospital ship, complete with beds for 20 intensive care patients and 94 medium dependency patients, plus facilities for up to 940 low-intensity patients. All three liners were at that time operated by the P&O line, who contributed heavily to the campaign. *Canberra* and *Queen Elizabeth 2* offered the advantage of being able to house large numbers of people in comfort; *Canberra* had a passenger capacity of 1,737 passengers plus 795 crew, many of whom were not needed for a spartan military transit, hence freed up their accommodation. *Queen Elizabeth 2* could take 1,892 passengers and 1,040 crew in peacetime.

But these great ships were just the tip of the iceberg. Many roll-on roll-off ferries were used to carry a mix of both troops and supplies, specifically *Elk*, *Europic Ferry*, *Norland*, *Nordic Ferry*, *Baltic Ferry* and *St Edmund*. *Elk*, for example, transported the Scimitars and Scorpions, three Sea King helicopters, tons of ammunition and eight 40mm Bofors

guns. *Norland*, which usually spent its time running passengers sedately between Hull and Rotterdam, carried 800 men of 2 Para plus men of 848 Naval Air Squadron (NAS). The many container/cargo ships and freighters in the STUFT fleet were similarly packed with supplies, the military taking advantage of huge commercial container spaces. The larger container/cargo ships tended to carry the Task Force's rotary assets, hence were of high value. The 27,867 GRT *Astronomer*, for example, carried no fewer than 13 helicopters, while *Atlantic Causeway* (14,946 GRT) transported eight Anti-Submarine Warfare (ASW) Sea Kings and 20 Westland Wessex helicopters. The *Atlantic Conveyor*, sister ship to *Causeway*, took an exceptional load – eight Sea Harriers, six Harriers, six Wessex and four Chinooks, the latter constituting the bedrock of the intended British airlift on the Falklands – therefore her loss to an Argentine Exocet missile on 25 May was a grievous blow. The seven freighters sent down to the South Atlantic tended to carry provisions, especially as some of the vessels had refrigeration facilities on board, while 15 accompanying civilian tankers were used as auxiliary support tankers, several with over-the-stern underwater refuelling equipment, to keep ships under power.

One interesting point to note about the sourcing of fuel was that, for fairly obvious political reasons, ships couldn't access refuelling facilities from ports on the South American coastline. Thus the main source of dockside refuelling was Freetown in Sierra Leone, Africa; its distance of 4,100 miles (6,600km) from the Falkland Islands explains the very high number of tankers employed in the Task Force.

A miscellany of small ships, many of them under 1,000 GRT, also found themselves on the Ministry of Defence's STUFT list. They were used in a range of capacities, including as tugs and as repair ships. One of the most impressive of the latter was the rapid conversion of the *Stena Seaspread* (6,061 GRT), a diving and oilfield support ship, which was refitted as a Task Force repair ship, subsequently conducting mid-ocean repairs to more than 50 vessels.

The STUFT ships were not simply requisitioned, turned over to different crews and sent back out to sea laden with military

personnel and supplies. Most actually retained their civilian crews, supplemented by Royal Navy parties in command and support. Most also underwent major engineering work to repurpose them and make them fit for military operations. A high number of the vessels all received helicopter pads, essential for the cross-decking of supplies and troops. This substantial fitting was not done under polished professional contracts, but was highly improvisational in nature, officers, engineers and air crews making the best judgement call about where to bolt a hefty metal platform on to the ship. The ships also received the fundamental kit and equipment to enable them to integrate into a naval fleet, such as the installation of military-spec communications and navigation systems. Many ships also acquired defensive armament, typically Oerlikon 20mm cannon bolted to available decks or pintle-mounted MAG machine guns attached to guard rails and other exposed points. Ships also had to be made more resistant to fire and combat damage, hence many of them had large

amounts of infrastructural materials – such as carpets and woodwork – either brutally removed or at least covered. A fine example of the scale of the engineering work is that of the *Canberra*, which acquired two helipads, each weighing between 70 and 90 tons, no mean feat on a ship with a light aluminium superstructure unsuited to taking the weight of the helipad, plus the fully loaded helicopter that sat on top of it. By such hasty innovations, however, the Task Force was able to acquire the logistical maritime muscle to make a distant war down in the Falklands a viable possibility.

Ascension Island

Were it not for Ascension Island, the British Task Force would have had to cope with an unbroken 8,000-mile (12,900km) distance between the UK and the Falkland Islands. As it was, Ascension Island provided what became an absolutely critical staging post at roughly the midway point.

As noted in Chapter 1, Ascension Island offered two welcome facilities of use to the Task Force – good anchorage for vessels in the roads off Georgetown, and also the excellent 10,000ft runway, which could take the biggest of military and civilian aircraft. Yet if these features would be maximised in value to support the Falklands campaign, there needed to be something of a revolution in terms of facilities development and logistical management. This revolution was largely performed by the tri-service British Forces Support Unit in Ascension Island (BFSUAI), commanded by Captain Robert McQueen. From an initial deployment of just a few dozen men, first landed on Ascension Island by C-130 Hercules on 3 April, the BFSUAI grew to be a force of approximately 1,000 soldiers, sailors and airmen.

Ascension Island performed five important functions in its logistical contribution to the Falklands War:

■ It acted as a staging post for Task Force vessels to take on fuel and supplies, or to

rationalise supplies already on board the vessels.

- It acted as a facility for holding stores.
- It served as the major logistical air hub between the UK and Falkland Islands, receiving inbound supply flights from the UK and facilitating outbound flights to the Falklands area.
- It provided limited onshore training and accommodation facilities for troops transiting between the UK and Falklands.
- It performed some essential administrative tasks for the Task Force fleet, such as handling incoming and outbound mail.

Central to the success of Ascension Island's logistical capacity was the development and efficient functioning of its air base. During peacetime, Wideawake Airfield handled around 200 civilian flights per year, but during war that figure leapt to, on occasions, up to 250 flights per day. The majority of these flights were resupply missions, bringing in endless streams of materiel and machines in the holds of C-130s, VC-10s and Boeing 707s. But there were also Nimrods performing long-range maritime surveillance sweeps out over the Atlantic. In addition, throughout the Falklands War, the Cold War continued unabated, and UK forces had to keep a close eye on Soviet long-range reconnaissance aircraft, submarines and surface vessels, which naturally took an interest in observing how the British would fight a professional land war. There was also the presence of 11 Victor bombers, operating as

air-to-air refuelling aircraft, plus for a short time the Vulcan bombers that delivered the 'Black Buck' raids over Stanley. Added to this were the constant helicopter flights to and from offshore vessels, ferrying supplies from shore to ship and vice versa.

The scale of the air operations is well summarised in an article written for *The*

Falklands War series of magazines published shortly after the conflict:

> By the time the Port Stanley was recaptured from the Argentines, a total of 535 air movements into the island airfield from Britain had taken place, including flights by RAF Hercules and VC10s, Belfasts chartered from Heavylift Air Cargo, and Boeing 707s chartered from British Airways and Tradewinds. These aircraft had delivered to Wideawake Airfield 23 helicopters, 5,242 passengers and nearly 6,000 tons of freight. The ground support personnel, including the original Pan Am staff, worked a small miracle in handling all this traffic, together with all aircraft operating to the south in support of the Task Force. Nimrod Maritime Surveillance aircraft flew 111 sorties from the island; C-130 Hercules made 44 airdrops of essential equipment, weapons and personnel to the Fleet; and the Victor K2 tankers supported 67 missions by flying 375 sorties to refuel in flight. Ground crew were able to keep these 20-year-old aircraft 100 per cent serviceable at all times – a remarkable achievement.[5]

BELOW A personal photograph of the Task Force under way, taken by Marine Andy Cole just before the assault on San Carlos. (Defence Picture Library)

Several points in this passage are worth commenting upon. First is the acknowledged role of the Americans in supporting the Ascension Island operations, particularly in their contributions to air traffic control. At the time of the conflict, American support for the British war effort was kept largely hidden, but it took some very visible forms at Ascension Island. US military and civilian logistics covertly supplied thousands of tons of supplies and fuel to the island. Almost all of the food that was supplied to the personnel on the island, for example, came courtesy of US Air Force C-141 transporters. The US Military Sealift Command also played its part in keeping the island's onshore fuel tanks filled with diesel and aviation fuel. By way of further example, during the Black Buck raids the BSFUAI had to cope with an unprecedented demand for aviation fuel, to supply no fewer than two Vulcan bombers and 11 Victor K2s for the operation, plus all the other aviation assets using Wideawake. The typical method of refuelling aircraft – bringing the fuel forward in bowsers from storage tanks 3.75 miles (6km) away – was inadequate, so RE personnel physically laid a pipeline from the storage tanks to the airfield. To prevent the storage tanks being depleted, however, US Navy fuel tankers simultaneously pumped the fuel ashore to replenish them.

While Task Force vessels weighed anchor off the coast of Ascension Island to take on supplies, there was also a highly efficient rotating system of helicopter resupply in operation, which enabled helicopters based on the island to restock passing ships without compelling them to stop. This was the system of 'vertical replenishment', or 'vertrep', and was primarily performed by Sea King, Wessex and Chinook helicopters. Underslung loads were prepared and flown out to nearby ships, to be lowered on to decks. Given the scale of the logistics involved, it was fast and highly pressurised work. In one day alone, the Joint Helicopter Support Unit – the main ground crew unit responsible for Ascension Island's helicopter logistics – deployed no fewer than 218 helicopter loads to offshore vessels.

Another important logistical system supporting the Task Force was that of the 'motorway stations', implemented once the

Total Exclusion Zone (TEZ) had been applied around the Falklands. These were essentially maritime resupply points, consisting of ships loaded with pre-requested supplies waiting at key locations to transfer those supplies to other ships. There were three such stations – one just off Ascension Island itself and also at latitudes 20 degrees and 40 degrees South.

Task Force departures and movements

The British Task Force did not sail south in one uniform deployment, but rather moved over a series of several weeks in rationalised formations. (Indeed, Task Force shipping was maintained from the UK throughout the conflict, not just in the initial days of deployment.) What was aptly termed the 'Advanced Group' departed between 29 March and 4 April, mainly from positions around the Mediterranean, these being ships redeployed from the Operation Springtrain exercise. The core of the Advanced Group was the initial deployment of nuclear submarines – specifically *Conqueror*, *Spartan* and *Splendid* – plus a collection of Royal Navy destroyers and frigates (*Antrim*, *Arrow*, *Brilliant*, *Coventry*, *Glamorgan*, *Plymouth* and *Sheffield*) and five ships from the RFA (*Appleleaf*, *Fort Austin*, *Sir Tristram*, *Tidespring* and *Typhoon*).

In the following week, from 5 to 11 April, the operational heart of the Task Force deployed in the form of the Carrier Battle Group (CVBG), centred around the carriers *Hermes* and *Invincible*, with their major air components. Accompanying combat vessels during this phase were the frigates *Alacrity*, *Antelope*,

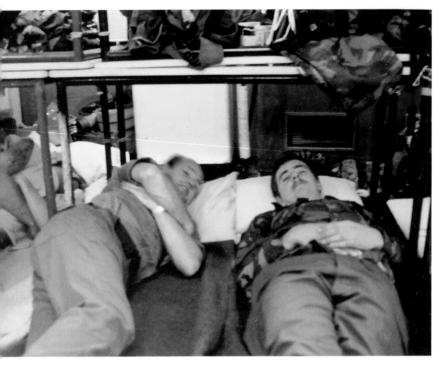

plus 3 Para. The combination of the assault ships, the fleet stores ship RFA *Stromness* and the *Canberra* composed the Amphibious Task Group (ATG).

Task Force departures in the week 12–15 April were mainly a small collection of merchant ships, including the *Stena Seaspread* and the *British Tamar*, plus the RFA fleet tanker *Blue Rover*, transporting fuel and dry goods. There were also some significant air movements to Ascension Island in the form of Victor K2s of 55 and 57 Squadrons and Nimrod MR.2s of 120, 201 and 206 Squadrons.

As the reality of combat appeared increasingly likely in the second half of April, the build-up of British ships in the Atlantic was reaching formidable proportions. During the week 19–25 April, the waters around Ascension Island became crowded with troop transports, amphibious ships and the LSL Group. Many of the soldiers had the brief opportunity to go ashore and conduct some physical exercise and weapons training at this time; seven firing ranges had been constructed on the island. Meanwhile, the CVBG and the Advanced Group had sailed on, rendezvousing north-east of the Falklands by 25 April. Note also that from the Advanced Group was detached the South Georgia Task Group, consisting of the destroyer *Antrim*, frigate *Plymouth*, Inshore Patrol Vessel (IPV) *Endurance*, the RFA *Tidespring*, plus a mixed force of M Coy, 42 Cdo, with SAS and SBS units. During this week, many new vessels also sailed from the UK to join the Task Force, including the frigates *Ardent* and *Argonaut* and the *Atlantic Conveyor*, *Europic Ferry* and RFA *Regent*. This was also the week in which the now-hospital ship *Uganda* departed from Gibraltar.

From 26 April to 2 May, now week five of the Task Force operations, the situation in the South Atlantic turned from diplomatic tensions into a shooting war, as the ships and the aircraft of the CVBG started to slug it out with attacking Argentine aircraft, plus the Argentine cruiser ARA *General Belgrano* was sunk in a submarine attack by HMS *Conqueror*. The bulk of the amphibious forces were still at Ascension Island, although the LSL Group was by now heading south, accompanied by the frigate *Antelope*. The momentum

ABOVE AND BELOW
Two photos from the personal collection of Andy Cole show fellow Marines getting their heads down aboard their transport ship. In the equatorial regions, the heat below decks was stifling. *(Andy Cole)*

Broadsword and *Yarmouth* and the Landing Platform Dock (LPD) HMS *Fearless*. There was also an extensive force of RFA vessels, including the four 'Sir' LSLs – *Sir Galahad*, *Sir Geraint*, *Sir Lancelot* and *Sir Percivale* (collectively these were known as the LSL Group). Most significant for the land campaign was the departure of several major troop-carrying merchant ships, including a heavily modified *Canberra*, which was transporting the men of 40 and 42 Cdo

behind the campaign meant that ships and aircraft were still streaming out of UK ports in significant numbers, and included the LPD HMS *Intrepid* (carrying Wessex and Sea King helicopters) plus five ships of the 11th Mine Countermeasures Squadron (11 MCMS).

In the first three weeks of May, running up to the British landings at San Carlos Water on 21 May, the Task Force naturally concentrated itself around the Falkland Islands, with the assault ships and LSL Group moving under the protective cover of the CVBG. The main ship movements from the United Kingdom during this time were principally cargo vessels and tankers, to feed the massive logistical demands of the combat operations, but there were also substantial shipments of helicopters and aircraft, including nine RAF Harrier GR.3s. The very last of the British ships to leave the UK before the onset of the land campaign were the RFA *Brambleleaf* and four transport vessels, the latter carrying one Sea King, two Wasps and three Chinooks.

The logistics of the Falklands War remains one of the most impressive feats of improvisation and organisation in modern military history. The rapidity with which the Task Force was assembled and deployed was little short of remarkable. What is sobering about this event is that, had the Argentines mounted the invasion of the Falkland Islands just a year later, Britain might conceivably not have had the capacity to have put together Operation Corporate.

ABOVE **The MV *Norland* was a P&O roll-on/roll-off ferry requisitioned by the MOD for the Falklands conflict, and used to transport and land a mixed force of Paras and Marines.** *(Griffiths 911; CC-BY-SA-4.0)*

RIGHT **Sea Harriers, Wessex helicopters and a Chinook on the deck of *Atlantic Conveyor*. The containers at the sides were stacked to create an 'open-top hangar'.** *(Defence Picture Library)*

Chapter Three

Air power operations

The outcome of the Falklands War, to a large extent, depended on the evolution of the war in the air. Argentine air attacks against Task Force shipping inflicted extremely high levels of loss on Royal Navy, RFA and merchant navy shipping, despite the best efforts of British surface-to-air missile (SAM) systems, anti-aircraft (AA) guns and carrier-borne fighter aircraft. Yet were it not for the achievements of Combat Air Patrol (CAP) missions performed by Fleet Air Arm (FAA) Sea Harriers, plus the many other contributions of British aircraft, rotary and fixed-wing, the British could have potentially suffered a defeat in the Falklands.

OPPOSITE The deck of HMS *Invincible* packed with Sea Harrier FRS.1s and Harrier GR.3s, which were flown by both RAF and RN pilots. *(Defence Picture Library)*

Of all the arms of service possessed by the Argentines, in many ways it was the Fuerza Aérea Argentina (Argentine Air Force) that concerned the British planners most at a strategic level. On the outbreak of war, the FAA had a total force of some 400 aircraft, about 200 of which were combat types. Added to this strength was that of the Comando de la Aviación Naval Argentina (CANA; Argentine Naval Air Command), which brought 130 aircraft to the table, most deployed from three mainland air bases but also a carrier-borne contingent aboard the *Veinticinco de Mayo*. The Argentine Army also had its own air component, principally logistical craft but including rotary vehicles with ground-attack capabilities, in the Comando de la Aviación del Ejército Argentina. The Prefectura Naval Argentina – essentially the Argentine coastguard – also brought minor aerial assets, mainly light reconnaissance and logistics types.

Argentine aircraft

Adding to the scale of the Argentine air forces was the modernity of many of its aircraft types. Unlike some Latin American states, Argentina had maintained a decent level of investment in both aircraft and training. Regarding the latter, Argentine pilots in early 1982 had no combat experience to speak of, but they had been well trained in France and Israel. The air forces in general also had a high state of morale, generally being spiritedly

nationalistic in outlook, flying with a passion that was borne out in the incredible courage displayed during repeated low-level combat passes over British shipping and through intense concentrations of AA fire and SAM barrages during the war.

The Argentines also possessed some excellent aircraft. Focusing principally on the combat types, the four main aircraft used were the Dassault Mirage IIIEA, the Israel Aircraft Industries (IAI) Dagger, the IA-58 Pucará ('Fortress') and the Douglas A-4 Skyhawk.

Taking these in order, the Mirage III was the most high-performance of the Argentine jets, a supersonic delta-wing fighter with a maximum speed of 1,460mph (2,350km/h) and a formidable armament of twin 30mm cannon, air-to-air missiles (AAMs) such as the Matra R.530 or Magic 1, air-to-surface missiles (ASMs) including rocket pods, plus up to 8,800lb (4,000kg) of payload on five external hardpoints, although these were often occupied by fuel drop tanks. The IAI Dagger was also of the Mirage family. It was essentially an Israeli copy of the Dassault Mirage 5 multirole fighter, which was basically a Mirage III but optimised for the Middle East export market. Performance of the Dagger was similar to that of the Mirage III.

The IA-58 Pucará, of which Argentina had 60 at the beginning of the war, was a radically different beast to the Mirage/Dagger. It was a low-wing, two-seat, twin-turboprop ground-attack and counter-insurgency aircraft, designed by Fábrica Militar de Aviones to carry a powerful array of two 20mm Hispano-Suiza HS.804, four 7.62mm FN Browning machine guns, and 3,570lb (1,620kg) of ordnance on external hardpoints. It was low-performance – maximum speed was 311mph (500km/h) at 9,842ft (3,000m) – but it was manoeuvrable and it could also take off from short, rough airfields, a fact that made it ideal for deployment to the Falklands.

The F-4 Skyhawk became one of the most familiar, and dreaded, silhouettes over the British Task Force during the Falklands conflict. The variants used by the Argentine air forces were the A-4B, A-4C and (by the Aviación Naval) the A-4Q. All were very dangerous opponents for the British forces. The Skyhawk was a subsonic aircraft, with a maximum

speed of around 673mph (1,083km/h), but with excellent manoeuvrability (aided by a very short wingspan) and the capacity for up to 9,900lb (4,490kg) of payload, which included AAMs, ASMs, bombs (cluster and unitary) and rocket pods, plus its integral twin 20mm cannon. The Skyhawk, a US design from McDonnell Douglas, had a proven combat history in Vietnam, and as delivered to the Argentines they included some sophisticated onboard fire-delivery systems.

These four aircraft were the centrepiece of the Argentine combat air components, but other systems also participated, some with notoriety. The most advanced aircraft in the Argentine inventory was the French Dassault-Breguet Super Étendard, designed as a carrier-borne strike fighter and operated in limited numbers by the Aviación Naval. Argentina received five Super Étendards in the second half of 1981, plus small quantities of the Exocet anti-ship missile that was intended to be the aircraft's main armament. The Super Étendard was also capable of carrying up to 4,600lb (2,100kg) or ordnance on external hardpoints, including AAMs, rocket pods and free-fall or laser-guided bombs (LGBs).

In ageing contrast, the Fuerza Aérea also operated 12 English Electric Canberras, purchased from the British during the 1970s. These twin-engine medium bombers – the first jet-powered bombers in the British air fleet – were by the time of the Falklands War a relic of the 1950s, and highly unsuited to operating in an environment of modern, manoeuvrable jet interceptors. Nevertheless, the Argentines deployed eight of the aircraft to Trelew air base, about 670 miles (1,078km) from the Falklands,

the intention being to use the Canberras for bombing runs against British ground troops.

The Argentines also supplemented their combat force with some trainer/light attack planes, aircraft that were typically outclassed in any battle for air superiority but which nevertheless added to the total force threat. These aircraft also had value for their ability to operate from short runways that were not viable for the faster jets. The two main types used directly from the Port Stanley air base were the Aermacchi MB-339, a dual-seat subsonic jet capable of handling up to 4,000lb (1,800kg) of external ordnance, including modern SAMs, and the turboprop Beechcraft T-34 Mentor, which had little utility apart from reconnaissance and very light strafing runs. Both of these types were operated by the naval air service.

In addition to the above, the Argentine air services operated a typically broad range of rotary and logistics aircraft.

Although both the Argentine aircraft, and their crews, were to be respected, there were nevertheless some faultlines running through the air services. There were issues with the serviceability of aircraft, especially regarding the availability of spare parts. Ground crews also had some gaps in their technical knowledge, especially in relation to using the Exocet from the Super Étendard, although this was substantially – and controversially – plugged by the presence of a nine-man French engineering team from Dassault, who arrived to help the Argentines in November 1981 and were still present in April 1982. Tactically and technically, both air and ground crew were also largely unfamiliar with the low-level, over-ground warfare that would characterise the Falklands air war, as evidenced by issues such as the incorrect fusing of bombs for low-level work.

But by far and away the biggest issues affecting the possibility of Argentine air superiority

was that of the capacity of the Falkland Islands' air facilities and the distance from mainland bases to the islands themselves. Although Stanley had a developed runway, it was not long enough to support Argentina's fast jets. Therefore, as noted in Chapter 2, these would have to fly from southern Argentine mainland bases, with a consequent drop in loiter, combat time and performance. For example, the greatest strength of the Mirage III when compared to the Sea Harrier was the former's supersonic speed. But that was only really achieved by engaging the aircraft's afterburners, which they couldn't do for reasons of fuel consumption – running the engines at full power would have used so much fuel that the aircraft likely wouldn't have been able to make it home.

Nevertheless, the fact remained that the Argentines had several air bases on the mainland within the combat radius of the Falkland Islands. These were:

Base*	Aircraft	Unit
BAN Almirante Zar (Trelew)	8 × Canberra B.Mk 62	Grupo 2 de Bombardeo
BAM Comodoro Rivadavia	Mirage IIIEA (small numbers)	Grupo 8 de Caza
	8 × IA-58 Pucará	Grupo 4 de Ataque
San Julián	10 × IAI Dagger	II/Grupo 6 de Caza
	15 × A-4C Skyhawk	Grupo 4 de Caza
BAM Rio Gallegos	26 × A-4B Skyhawk	Grupo 5 de Caza
	10 × Mirage IIIEA	Grupo 8 de Caza
BAN Rio Grande	10 × IAI Dagger	III/Grupo 6 de Caza
	5 × Super Étendard	2 Escuadrilla de Caza y Ataque
	8 × A-4Q Skyhawk	3 Escuadrilla de Caza y Ataque

* BAN = Base Aérea Naval; BAM = Base Aérea Militar

Taken together, therefore, the Argentines had just over 100 mainland-based combat aircraft with the operational range to conduct missions over the Falkland Islands and the surrounding waters.

On the Falkland Islands themselves, there were three main air bases for the Argentines, principally devoted to ground-attack capabilities. Port Stanley offered the most substantial air facilities on the islands, with its 4,100ft (1,250m) asphalt runway. The air base was redesignated BAM Malvinas by the Fuerza Aérea Argentina, although it also shared the facility with some naval units, who called it Estación Aeronaval (EAN) Malvinas. The other main base was BAM Condor, at Goose Green, and EA Calderón on Pebble Island. Between these three, by late April, was distributed the force of aircraft that included the following:

Base	Aircraft	Unit
BAM Malvinas; BAM Condor; EA Calderón	24 × IA-58 Pucará	Grupo 3 de Ataque
BAM Malvinas	6 × Aermacchi MB-339A	1 Escuadrilla de Ataque
BAM Malvinas; EA Calderon	4 × Beech T-43C-1	3 Escuadrilla de Ataque
BAM Condor	2 × Bell Model 212 helicopters	Grupo 7 de Coin Escuadron
BAM Condor	2 × CH-47C Chinook helicopters	Grupo 7 de Coin Escuadron
BAM Malvinas	2 × Shorts Skyvan	Prefectura Naval Argentina
BAM Malvinas	1 × Aérospatiale Puma helicopter	Prefectura Naval Argentina
Moody Brook	Multiple army helicopters	Batallón de Aviación de Combate 601

Although many of the helicopters listed here were given light armament, their main role was that of providing cross-island logistics for both the air services and the ground troops. As is evident from the list, however, the Argentine air forces on the Falklands themselves were in no way configured to establish any sort of local air superiority.

British air assets

This chapter is primarily focused upon combat aviation in the Falklands; that is, those aircraft devoted either to air defence, bombing or ground-attack duties. The pivotal combat aircraft in the Task Force was, of course, the Sea Harrier, deployed aboard the carriers *Hermes* and *Invincible*. For the first stages of the campaign, *Hermes* deployed 12 Sea Harriers from the Fleet Air Arm's No. 800 HQ Training Squadron and No. 809 Naval Air Squadron (NAS), and eight for *Invincible* from No. 801 NAS. These assets were reinforced from mid-May by eight more Sea Harriers from No. 809 NAS, plus four RAF Harrier GR.3s from No. 1 Squadron, the latter initially deployed to *Hermes* but later transferred to ground bases, once secured.

Because of the location of the conflict (well beyond the range of any British-owned land bases), and the reliance on carrier deployment, the Sea Harrier was the perfect solution for air defence over the islands. Although a subsonic aircraft – its maximum speed was 735mph (1,182km/h) – the Sea Harrier had good acceleration and superb manoeuvrability. Its defining characteristic were its four vectorable jet nozzles (two each side of the fuselage), which could control the direction of thrust from the single Rolls-Royce Pegasus 103 turbofan engine. This feature made it V/STOL capable – Vertical/Short Take-Off and Landing – which was crucial for the Falklands ops, as it meant that the Sea Harriers could take off from the carriers in rough weather without the carrier having to wing around into the wind to raise take-off windspeed. The Sea Harrier could also perform an air combat manoeuvre known as 'viffing'. This could be executed if an enemy was attacking from behind the Sea Harrier, and involved the pilot suddenly angling the jet nozzles downward, resulting in a very sudden braking and climbing effect that effectively punched the Sea Harrier up and out of the attacker's alignment; the attacker would then overshoot the Harrier, at which point the Sea

BELOW The Sea Harrier's V/STOL capability meant that it could still operate from carrier decks already packed with helicopters and other aircraft.

Harrier pilot would again rotate the jet nozzles to the rear to apply forward thrust, this time chasing the attacker from behind in a sudden role reversal. It should be noted, however, that the 'viffing' characteristic appears to have been seldom used during the Falklands War, despite the excited coverage that it received from the press at the time. In fact, most of the air kills were achieved through more conventional air combat manoeuvres, albeit ones superbly and innovatively applied by the well-trained British pilots, who undoubtedly made the best tactical use of the vectorable thrust system.

In addition to its manoeuvrability, the Sea Harrier also offered a superb spectrum of defensive and offensive technologies. In addition to its standard two 30mm ADEN cannon pods, the aircraft could carry an 8,000lb (3,630kg) payload. For ground attack, this could include free-fall bombs and laser-guided Precision Guided Munitions (PGMs), plus Matra rocket pods with 18 SNEB 68mm rockets per pod. For air-to-air defence, the Sea Harriers were armed with the AIM-9L Sidewinder, the latest version of this state-of-the-art AAM. What was critically different about this AAM compared to previous versions was its 'all-aspect' engagement profile, meaning that it could be fired at enemy aircraft

regardless of their position in relation to the missile; the missile could even be launched at opponents directly behind. This weapon, allied with the Ferranti Blue Fox multi-role airborne radar (introduced into the FAA in 1981), was a proficient killer in air combat, although the lack of 'look-down' capability in the Blue Fox system meant that pilots always had to fly the aircraft aggressively – the technology never fought the battle for itself. Also note that the Sea Harriers

ABOVE Sea Harriers and GR.3s on the deck of *Hermes*.

BELOW Sea Harriers aboard HMS *Invincible*, accompanied by the Type 22 frigate HMS *Battleaxe*. (Defence Picture Library)

SEA HARRIER/HARRIER SERVICEABILITY

The Sea Harrier/Harrier platform was, among its many virtues, incredibly tough, resistant to all manner of hard use, reliable in airframe, powerplant and avionics and able to absorb a significant amount of battle damage and stay operational. In fact, almost all the Harrier-type aircraft used in the campaign were hit by small-arms fire at some point, but only when the strikes were from heavier-calibre weapons (20mm and above) and missiles did impacts translate into combat losses. Yet although the aircraft themselves were creditably strong, further acclamation must also go to the maintenance teams who kept the aircraft operational under the most demanding of theatre conditions. This job was made far harder by the loss of *Atlantic Conveyor*. In addition to the aircraft and vehicle losses aboard this ship, the vessel was also home to a large and well-equipped aircraft maintenance centre for performing major structural repairs on aircraft, with extensive spare parts stores. Technicians from the Royal Navy's Mobile Aircraft Repair Transport and Salvage Unit (MARTSU) were aboard to conduct this work. With the loss of the ship, the MARTSU personnel plus the squadron Aircraft Engineer Officers (AEOs) and general ground crew had to rely on improvisation and limited parts stores to keep the aircraft flying, which they did impressively with very little downtime.

BELOW RAF C-130 Hercules aircraft played a major role in supporting airhead to Ascension. It was also planned to use the aircraft in an SAS raid into Argentina itself; the raid was later sensibly cancelled. In the foreground is one of the Black Buck Vulcans, which is carrying a Shrike anti-radar missile on an underwing pylon.

were equipped, for defensive purposes, with both chaff and flare dispensers, both of which proved useful in the short-range actions over the Falklands.

As well as the Sea Harriers, standard RAF GR.3 Harriers were deployed to the Falklands later in the campaign, initially with a view to being replacements for the expected air losses. As it turned out, the RAF Harriers were put to full use in their classic ground-attack role, relieving some FAA aircraft from this duty and allowing them to gravitate more back towards the air defence role.

In terms of fixed-wing aircraft, the other big combat player in the Falklands War – albeit one that had only few visible actions – was the Vulcan B.2. This nuclear-capable Cold War strategic bomber was, and remains, instantly recognisable, with its inspiring delta-wing configuration. When the Falklands conflict began in April 1982, the Vulcan was effectively in its decline phase, the B.2 having been in service since 1960. At the height of its use, five air bases had hosted a total of nine squadrons, but by 1982 just three squadrons were left – 44, 50 and 101 – all at RAF Waddington. Nevertheless, the unique requirements of the Falklands War tapped into two of the Vulcan's primary virtues: 1) its long-range capability, with a maximum range of 2,607 miles (4,171km) – dramatically extendable through air-to-air refuelling and 2) its heavy conventional ordnance load of 21 × 1,000lb bombs. It was these capabilities that led to the famous, and controversial, 'Black Buck' raids (see below).

Another large part played in the Falklands air war, albeit one often overlooked, was that of British rotary-wing aircraft; that is, the helicopters of the FAA, the Army Air Corps (AAC), Royal Marines and Royal Air Force (RAF). The chief helicopters deployed to the Falklands were as follows:

Fleet Air Arm
- Sea King (814, 820, 824, 825, 826, 846 Naval Air Squadrons)
- Wessex (737, 845, 847, 848 Naval Air Squadrons)
- Lynx (815 Naval Air Squadron)
- Wasp (829 Naval Air Squadron)

Army Air Corps/Royal Marines
- Scout (3 Commando Brigade Air Squadron RM, 656 Squadron AAC)
- Gazelle (3 Commando Brigade Air Squadron RM, 656 Squadron AAC)

Royal Air Force
- Sea King (202 Squadron).

In FAA service, the Sea King was primarily used to provide ASW cover, Helicopter Delivery Service (HDS)/VERTREP sorties – moving logistics and personnel – and Search-and-Rescue (SAR) missions. The RAF Sea Kings performed exactly the same roles, with the omission of the ASW function. The naval Wessex helicopters were primarily used for HDS and VERTREP. All helicopters at some point during the conflict also found themselves involved in casualty evacuation (CASEVAC).

The Lynx HAS.2 helicopter was principally a combat type, being equipped with the Sea Skua ASM for engaging surface vessels and the Stingray torpedo and depth charges for destroying submarines. The naval Lynx spent much of their time performing ASW patrols around the Task Force, but they also

ABOVE *Invincible*'s 'ski-jump' deck facility converted forward motion into a positive rate of climb for the aircraft; such facilities are typically fitted to carriers that do not have catapult launch. *(Defence Picture Library)*

BELOW A Sea King puts down on the helideck that had been improvised on the stern deck of the liner SS *Canberra*. *(Defence Picture Library)*

made numerous logistical flights, plus were
roughly adapted for the helicopter gunship
role; a GPMG was fitted to the helicopter
door during the journey south, the improvised
mount consisting of the lower part of an office
swivel chair, turned upside down and affixed
to the rim of the door! The Lynx was actually
the gradual replacement for the light Wasp
HAS.1 helicopter, although at the time of
the Falklands War many Wasps were still in
service, performing largely the same anti-ship
and ASW roles as the larger Lynx, plus light
reconnaissance duties.

For the land forces, the main rotary support
came from the Scout and the Gazelle (plus
logistical assistance from the one Chinook
helicopter – the infamous 'Bravo November'
– which survived the sinking of the *Atlantic
Conveyor*). The diminutive Scout AH.1 was
essentially either a general utility helicopter or,
when armed with SS.11 anti-tank missiles, an
anti-tank guided weapon (ATGW) platform.
The larger (five-seat) Gazelle also had utility
roles, but also offered capabilities for ground
attack, ATGW warfare, SF liaison, aerial artillery
direction and reconnaissance. Specifically in the
Falklands conflict, the Gazelle was fitted with
the 68mm SNEB rocket pods, although these
were actually little used in combat.

The 'Black Buck' raids

The first 'Black Buck' raid of 1 May 1982
was arguably the most high-profile British
air operation of the Falklands War, albeit one
subsequently dogged with no small measure
of controversy and critique. The mission
proposition was ostensibly simple – RAF
Vulcans would mount a long-range bombing
raid against BAM Malvinas at Port Stanley,
damaging the runway to such an extent that
it would be unable to host any advanced jet
aircraft, or expand its existing contingent of air
assets. There were some question marks over
the operation at the outset. The first was the
state of the Vulcan fleet at this time.

As the Vulcan fleet, based exclusively
at RAF Waddington, wound down toward
obsolescence, its level of serviceability for
an ultra-long-range operation against the
Falkland Islands was open to question. The
key challenge was that of refuelling. Although,
as a strategic bomber, the Vulcans had a
decent maximum range, the distance from
Ascension Island (the nearest base from which
the operation could be launched) was still 3,800
miles (6,100km); just a one-way trip would be
well beyond the Vulcan's standard range. So,
to launch the operation, a complex air-to-air

refuelling process had to be developed. This was made more complicated by the fact that although the Vulcans had refuelling probes, they basically hadn't been used in about a decade, and had to be brought up to operational standards. There was an accompanying frantic hunt for spare parts no longer being manufactured; one Vulcan refuelling connector was tracked down to an officer's mess, where it was in use as an ashtray. Crews also had to be trained rapidly to perform air-to-air refuelling.

There was also the question as to what the Vulcans could actually achieve for this intensive investment of resources. Runways are notoriously difficult structures to damage in anything other than temporary fashion; even deep craters can be filled and tarmacked over quite quickly by a motivated damage-control crew. Yet if any aircraft could do it, it was the Vulcan. Its bombload dwarfed that of the Sea Harrier – the only other aircraft capable of attacking the Stanley air base – and it could potentially achieve more in a single pass than multiple Sea Harriers could impose in multiple sorties, during which missions the air defences would become increasingly alert and proficient. Also, there was the psychological impetus for the RAF to make a contribution to the campaign that was, to date, dominated by the

Army, Navy and Royal Marines. Thus it was that on 30 April Operation Black Buck received the green light.

The plan for the attack was an ornate choreography involving a total of 13 aircraft: 2 Vulcan B.2s (XM607 – Flight Lieutenant Martin Withers; XM598 – Squadron Leader John Reeve), plus 11 Victor K.2 refuelling aircraft, the Vulcans having deployed from Waddington to Wideawake on 29 April. In basic outline, the formation of 13 aircraft would head out for the Falklands, the Victors performing a sequence of fuel transfers both to the Vulcans and to each other, each Victor turning back for Ascension Island as it was emptied, leaving diminishing numbers of the tankers to get the Vulcans to their objective. It was ambitious and finely balanced.

Having been given the go-ahead, the 13 aircraft began taking off from Wideawake from 23:50hrs on 30 April, for secrecy doing so in complete darkness with all runway and navigation lights turned off. The challenges stacked up when, a short way into the flight, a problem with XM598's direct vision window was discovered, meaning that the aircraft could not pressurise; it was therefore forced to turn back, leaving XM607 to perform the bomb run on its own.

The refuelling schedule initially went to plan, the numbers of Victors in the flight steadily

ABOVE The Vulcan bomber was, even in 1982, something of a relic of the 'V-bomber' age. It required extensive modification (particularly in terms of AAR) and crew training to revisit its conventional bombing role in the Falklands. This historic photograph shows Vulcan XM607 touching down at Wideawake airfield on 1 May 1982, 16 hours and 2 minutes after delivering its attack on the airfield at Port Stanley.

AIR-TO-AIR REFUELLING

The following account relates an episode from the first operational C-130 air-to-air refuel in the South Atlantic, as told by Squadron Leader (then Flight Lieutenant) Harry Burgoyne AFC RAF (Retd):

The slim, elegant shape of the Victor swiftly overtook the ungainly Hercules, stabilised itself just forward of the Hercules' right wing and, on Rowley's command, both aircraft began a gradual descent of about 500ft per minute. Trying to keep my control inputs to a minimum, I carefully manoeuvred into a line astern position about 20ft behind the Victor's trailing refuelling hose and began my hook-up run. Under Bob's calm directions, and with the engineer monitoring the engines, the two giants slowly closed until the refuelling probe on top of the Hercules and the Victor's dancing basket were only 10ft apart. AAR [air-to-air refuelling] has been described as 'trying to spear a rolling doughnut' and this was no exception. Time and again, I edged my aircraft forward but each time failed to get the probe into the basket. Although I was getting frustrated with my inability to find the target, I had to put that aside and keep on trying, but I was conscious that valuable fuel was being used up and the formation was getting lower and lower. Finally, as we passed through 17,000ft and with my self-induced pressure becoming almost unbearable, at the sixth attempt a successful contact was made and fuel began to flow.

Transferring the required 37,000lb of fuel took 30 minutes and, towards the end, it was a real touch-and-go situation. By that time, both aircraft had descended to around 2,500ft and we were dodging around the cumulonimbus clouds that I had assessed earlier as not being a problem![1]

reducing until just two were left accompanying the remaining Vulcan. Then a refuelling hook-up between the two Victors went awry in turbulence, and one aircraft suffered a damaged fuel-receiving probe. This resulted in one of the Victors having to return early, and the remaining Victor later having to transfer more fuel to the Vulcan than the Victor actually needed for the return trip to Ascension Island. It would have to rely upon an emergency refuelling about 450 miles (724km) out from Ascension, a nail-biting prospect as the strict conditions of radio silence meant it would not be able to communicate with Ascension until it was close. Nevertheless, the priority was to keep XM607 on its mission.

At a distance of 300 miles (483km) from the target, XM607 dropped down to an altitude of just 300ft (91m) over the sea, to reduce the risk of detection by the Argentine air defence radar. Then, at 40 miles (64km) from Stanley, Withers pulled the aircraft up to its bomb-run altitude of 10,000ft (3,048m), setting the aircraft on a heading of 235 degrees, so that the bombs would fall in a roughly diagonal line across the runway, maximising the chances of at least one hit. Bomb release took place 3 miles (5km) from the runway, the Vulcan then turning back, the crew amazed at the complete lack of AA response from the Argentines, partly the result of Argentine inefficiency and partly that of the Vulcan's air electronics officer jamming the Skyguard gun-control radar. Of the 21 bombs dropped, one – the first bomb of the stick – made a large crater in the centre of the runway at the midpoint. The others ran through aircraft dispersal areas and storage facilities, causing substantial damage, including one Pucará aircraft destroyed; XM607 returned home safely after nearly 16 hours in the air.

Although the most famous of the 'Black Buck' raids, 'Black Buck 1' was actually the first of seven such attacks, both conventional bombing runs and also attacks against the Argentine air-defence surveillance radar using AGM-45 Shrike anti-radiation missiles. In summary, these missions were as follows:

LEFT The sizeable crater left by a 1,000lb bomb, dropped around Stanley from a Vulcan 'Black Buck' raid. *(Pettebutt/PD-self)*

Raid no.	Date	Principal aircraft/mission	Results
Black Buck 2	3–4 May	XM607 Attack on BAM Malvinas at Port Stanley; bomb run at 16,000ft (4,877m)	No bomb strikes on runway
Black Buck 3	13 May	XM598, XM607 Attack on BAM Malvinas at Port Stanley	Raid cancelled following maintenance issues
Black Buck 4	28–29 May	XM597 Shrike anti-radar mission, Port Stanley	Raid aborted mid-flight due to problems with lead Victor HDU failure
Black Buck 5	30–31 May	XM597 Shrike anti-radar mission, Port Stanley	Minor damage to the Westinghouse AN/TPS-43F radar operated by Grupo 2 de Vigilancia y Control; radar operational within 24 hours
Black Buck 6	2–3 June	XM597 Shrike anti-radar mission, Port Stanley	Ejercito-operated Cardion TPS-44 radar (controlling GASA601 AA batteries) destroyed by two Shrikes; refuelling issues resulted in the Vulcan diverting to Rio de Janeiro
Black Buck 7	11–12 June	XM607 Bombing missions against Stanley airport facilities	Significant infrastructural damage inflicted

Posterity has not been too kind to the Black Buck raids, as some have argued that the vast expenditure of resources (especially numbers of aircraft involved, airframe/component hours and fuel) did not justify the limited destruction imposed upon the enemy. The subject continues to be the source of ongoing argument, but in the same way that a sniper's results are not just measured in the number of kills, but also in the operational limits he places upon the enemy, the Black Buck raids had effects far beyond shell craters and destroyed equipment. The raids proved to the Argentines that the British had the reach, and therefore the option, of strategic bomber strikes against the mainland, resulting in many of the Argentine Mirage fighters being deployed to air bases in the north of the country, rather than to the southern airfields where they could have been of use to the Falklands air campaign. With the introduction of the Shrike anti-radar missions, furthermore, the Argentine air defence operators had to exercise greater caution, frequently switching off their radars to prevent detection, and thereby creating a safer (though never entirely safe) operating environment for all British combat aircraft. Finally, the raids meant that the Argentines had to put in place numerous measures to counter strategic bombing attacks, further dispersing the focus and energy required to engage multiple other threats.

Air-to-air combat

It is a fact that the British never achieved air superiority over the Falkland Islands – at least not until the very final days of the war. Argentine air assaults continued to be a threat throughout the conflict, and the significant numbers of British ships sunk is testimony to the fact that control of the airspace was always contested. The primary reason for this is statistical – the Task Force could never deploy sufficient aircraft to take full control of the skies, especially not

BELOW A Bomb Damage Assessment (BDA) intelligence photograph taken by a Canberra, showing damage inflicted by a 'Black Buck' Vulcan strike against Stanley airport. *(Defence Picture Library)*

with the enemy able to draw upon their full air force based on the mainland. Thus the FAA flyers alone flew a prodigious number of hours just to maintain the CAP – 2,782 flying hours in total, an extraordinary figure given the limited number of aircraft and the relatively short combat short radius involved. (Transport aircraft, by contrast, flew 7,719 hours, but these journeys included the shuttles between the UK and Ascension Island.)

Despite the disparity in numbers between Argentine and British combat aircraft, however, the British fighter pilots helped make the airspace over the Falklands very hostile indeed. In fact, while in air-to-air combat the Sea Harriers destroyed or seriously damaged 21 Argentine aircraft, the Argentine air forces managed to inflict no similar losses in return. Such a combat record is a profound testimony to the skills and aircraft of the FAA.

The first major day of air-to-air combat over the Task Force was 1 May, the day on which the first Black Buck raid made its strike on Port Stanley air base. Shortly after this action, a unit of Sea Harriers made a low-level strike on the same target, attacking through clouds of AA fire at low level to deploy 1,000lb (454kg) bombs (air burst and delayed action), plus BL755 cluster bombs. In response, Dagger As of Grupo 6 and Mirage IIIEAs of Grupo 8 responded, flying in at moderate speed of 550mph (885km/h) and high, at about 34,450ft (10,500m), obviously intending to launch an

attack on the Task Force shipping; at this time, naval gunfire support (NGS) was hitting Port Stanley. At a distance of about 120 miles (193km), six incoming aircraft were detected by HMS *Invincible*'s radar and the details relayed to a two-man Sea Harrier CAP from No. 801 Squadron, the lead Sea Harrier flown by Flight Lieutenant Paul Barton and that of his wingman by Lieutenant Commander John Eyton-Jones. The two Sea Harriers, despite being significantly outnumbered, were vectored in to the intercept.

The tactical decisions began even as the two sets of aircraft approached at distance. The Argentine jets maintained their altitude, aware that their best advantages against the highly manoeuvrable Sea Harriers came from height and speed. Both sides stuck to their defensive positions, while attempting to manoeuvre out of the range of each other's missiles. Eventually the Argentine jets were compelled to turn back, as they ran low on fuel.

The day's events were far from over. Shortly afterwards, two Sea Harriers intercepted and engaged three T-34C-1 aircraft heading to strafe the NGS vessels off Stanley; cannon shots were fired, but the light attack aircraft managed to escape to the AA umbrella over Stanley, courtesy of some fortuitous thick fog. But then, in the later part of the afternoon, the Daggers and Mirages returned in greater force; augmented by some Canberra bombers of Grupo 2, the total number of aircraft was about 20. Once again, Barton was flying the CAP, this time accompanied by Lieutenant Steve Thomas on the wing. They encountered two aircraft of the incoming force – Mirage IIIEAs of Grupo 8, piloted by Captain Garcia Cuerva and (as wingman) Lieutenant Carlos Perona – apparently flying their mission independently, as no other Argentine aircraft could be detected in the vicinity. While Thomas flew in towards the threat head-on, Barton made a wide swing out to the right to flank the two incoming jets, which appeared to be oblivious to his manoeuvre, even after Barton fired an opportunistic stream of 30mm cannon rounds at them. Barton fastened his attention on Perona's Mirage, and closed on the enemy's tail while the Sidewinder achieved lock-on, indicated by its distinctive auditory 'growl'. He fired the missile:

BELOW An Argentine Super Étendard strike fighter pictured at Tierra del Fuego; all such aircraft flew from mainland bases. *(Defence Picture Library)*

LEFT An Argentine Mirage jet flies low and fast on an attack run over LSL *Sir Bedivere* in San Carlos Water in the early days of the Task Force landings. *(Defence Picture Library)*

At first I thought it had failed. It came off the rail and ducked down. I had not fired a 'winder before so its behaviour at launch was new to me. I was surprised not to see it home straight in – to see it duck down was disconcerting. I'd begun to wonder if it was a dud. It took about half a mile for it to get its trajectory sorted out, then it picked itself up and for the last half a mile it just homed straight in. The missile flight time was about four seconds, then the Mirage exploded in a brilliant blue, orange and red fireball.[2]

Perona managed to eject and escape.

Thomas, meanwhile, was engaged in a fast turning competition with Cuerva, who was now breaking for cloud cover. The Sea Harrier managed, via a roll, to get into a good lock-on position and Thomas released one of his Sidewinders. In thick cloud, out of sight of Thomas, the Sidewinder exploded via the missile's proximity fuse, detonating the 22lb (10kg) annular-blast fragmentary warhead and causing serious damage to the Mirage. The unlucky Cuerva attempted to wrest his aircraft back to BAM Malvinas, but the act of releasing his drop tanks near to the air base prior to an emergency landing convinced Argentine gunners that he was an enemy aircraft dropping bombs, and they thus shot him out of the sky, killing the brave pilot.

The first two British air-to-air kills had been made, and more followed quickly. A Sea Harrier from No. 800 Squadron, flown by Flight Lieutenant Tony Penfold, shot down one of two Daggers from Grupo 6, then minutes later Lieutenant Al Curtiss of No. 801 Squadron shot down one of two Canberra B.Mk 62 bombers from Grupo 2. Both kills were again made with Sidewinder missiles. One of the No. 800 Sea Harriers had a fraught few seconds being pursued by an AAM fired by one of the Daggers, but there were no British casualties.

The astonishing first day of kills largely set the pattern of Sea Harrier successes during the Falklands War. The overwhelming majority of the kills against fast jets were made using the AIM-9L Sidewinder, which exhibited an 80% kill-to-launch ratio. The AIM-9L itself had undergone some significant improvements over

BELOW Many of the Sea Harrier interceptions of Argentine aircraft were vectored in by personnel aboard naval destroyers and frigates. *(Defence Picture Library)*

the previous versions, not only the 'all-aspect ratio' mentioned earlier, but also an improved detector element, modified canards to give better aerial manoeuvrability and more accurate proximity detonation through an improved active laser fuse. Combined with the capabilities of the Sea Harrier platform, it was a compelling prospect.

Kills therefore came thick and fast, not least when the Sea Harriers found themselves in the thick of the action countering the Argentine air strikes against Task Force and Amphibious Group shipping following the San Carlos landings. In contrast to the early Mirage/Dagger encounters, this action was all at low level, and principally against the versatile and more manoeuvrable A-4 Skyhawk. Still, the Sea Harrier pilots largely managed to get the measure of the attackers. For example, in the mid-afternoon of 21 May, two No. 800 Squadron Sea Harriers from HMS *Hermes*, flown by Lieutenant Commander Neil Thomas and Lieutenant Commander Mike Blissett, were on a CAP over Falkland Sound, at first to intercept an A-4B Skyhawk of Grupo 5 that had attempted to bomb *Ardent*. Although the British pilots could not locate this target, they suddenly came across three A-4Cs of Grupo 4 heading over West Falkland to San Carlos Water. Despite the fact that the Skyhawk

pilots spotted the Sea Harriers, and attempted evasive manoeuvres, both Blissett and Thomas achieved lock-on with their Sidewinders, resulting in two kills. Blissett also appears to have damaged a third Skyhawk with a burst of 30mm ADEN cannon fire.

This was one of several incidents in which single Sea Harrier CAPs destroyed multiple Argentine aggressors. The attrition, furthermore, continued until late in the conflict. One of the most spectacular actions occurred on Tuesday 8 June, when four A-4B Skyhawks of Grupo 5 ran into a CAP flown by Flight Lieutenant David Morgan and Lieutenant D. Smith over Bluff Cove. Morgan has recounted the episode in detail, which takes us to the heart of the intensely rapid decision-making that characterises modern air combat:

We had been there about 45 or 50 minutes I suppose – there were two of us. Fuel was getting quite low, the carrier [Hermes] was quite a long way out, and it was starting to get dark. We had lost the option of going into the tin strip at San Carlos, because it was getting dark – there was no way of getting in there; there were no lights on the strip. Looking down I noticed one of our small landing craft coming around from Choiseul Sound and heading up toward

BELOW A Sea Harrier prepares for a CAP sortie; note the AIM-9L Sidewinder visible beneath the starboard wing. *(Defence Picture Library)*

the rest of the ships burning in Bluff Cove, and in the turn I looked down and saw an aircraft about 300 yards short of this ship, obviously going in to attack it. I just yelled out that I'd seen something and dived down after it from about 10,000ft. I saw the lead aircraft attack the landing craft and miss it. I then saw a second aircraft running in for the attack and decided to take him first. I was still accelerating down the hill, still 4 or 5 miles away at this stage, and I saw him hit the back of the ship with a bomb of some sort. There was a large explosion so I knew that he'd done a lot of damage and probably killed a lot of people. At that stage I started to get very angry.

I was converting onto his tail and was almost within firing range when I saw out of the corner of my left eye a third aircraft, which would have been in a position to threaten me if I hadn't gone in for him first. So I pulled my aircraft across to the left, and at this stage we were probably down to around 100ft above the water going much faster than the Harrier was ever designed to go. I locked my port missile onto him and fired it. Just the missile coming off the rails threw my aircraft over onto the right wingtip past the vertical, which was a hell of a shock, but the missile went straight up his jet pipe and blew him to pieces. Very, very little debris of any sort hit the water – it was very small bits. Within about four or five seconds I'd lined the other missile up and locked it on to the guy in front, the No. 2, and fired at him. He'd seen the first guy explode and was turning gently back left to find out what was going on I guess, and I think he saw my missile come off – it makes quite a lot of smoke. He then broke right and tried to run away, which is exactly the right thing to do, but I was going a lot faster than he was and I was fairly close, and the missile just took the back of his aircraft off completely; it hit just behind the cockpit and the back end of the aircraft disappeared totally. The canopy and the front of the cockpit then rotated through about 90 degrees and went straight into the water within about half a second; he was down about 50 or 60ft at this stage and I was only slightly higher. I felt

great exhilaration at this stage having got two of them. I was then running through for the front aircraft, which was running very low, out to the southwest. At this stage the second guy I'd shot down – the one who had hit the landing craft – actually managed to get out of the aircraft, using his [ejection] seat and the parachute opened right in front of me, in fact it nearly went down my intake – he went just over the left-hand wing. I then went forward for the remaining Skyhawk, which was running up towards Goose Green. Unfortunately as I had fired my second Sidewinder the head-up display – which has all the weapon-aiming symbology on it – went out, so I just had a black windscreen, no gunsight. So I flew in to about 300 or 400 yards and tried to hit the A-4 with guns, and missed, unfortunately.

Meanwhile my No. 2 had seen my two explosions – he hadn't seen the target aircraft at all – and then suddenly saw another aircraft flying very low across the water, with explosions all around it, and he thought that someone was firing at me. He called for me to break up out of the way. I at that stage had run out of bullets so pulled up vertically; he saw me go up and realised that the aircraft he'd just seen was a target. So he locked it with one of his Sidewinders and fired, and got the third one. The fourth one got away to take the story home. We then discovered that we were desperately short of fuel, and spent 30-odd very anxious minutes on the way back to Hermes, and landed with a couple of minutes' fuel remaining. Luckily they had kept the bar open for us, so we both had a couple of well-earned pints![3]

This three-aircraft kill mission was an extraordinary event in the last acts of the air war during the Falklands. The only Argentine aircraft shot down after this incident was a Canberra B.Mk 62 of Grupo 2, which on 13 June was hit by a Sea Dart fired from HMS Exeter.

As mentioned earlier, the vast majority of the kills were achieved with Sidewinders, although the 30mm ADEN cannon was also applied to good effect; on 21 May alone, one Skyhawk was shot down and another damaged by accurate 30mm bursts. When we add the

huge volume of SAM and AA fire from British ships and shore batteries, the skies above the Falklands became one of the most hostile places in the world for combat pilots.

We should also mention that the Sea Harriers, and RAF Harriers, did not just engage fixed-wing jets, but also imposed some high kill rates on Argentine logistical and rotary-wing aircraft. Indeed, prior to his impressive Skyhawk interdiction in June, Flight Lieutenant Morgan alone had notched up several helicopter kills.

On 23 May, Morgan and his wingman, John Leeming, were conducting a CAP from *Hermes* over West Falkland when they spotted four Argentine helicopters at low level – three Pumas and an A-109A Hirundo gunship – making a supply flight from Port Stanley to Port Howard. Morgan made a fast cannon pass, with the unexpected result that one of the panicking Puma pilots flew his aircraft into the ground; the crew managed to bail out of the wrecked aircraft before it caught fire and exploded. (Note that Sidewinders are better suited to engaging fast, fixed-wing aircraft, rather than slow and terrain-hugging rotary aircraft.) The other helicopters scattered, but the Sea Harriers went hunting them. The A-109A was discovered, abandoned by its crew, sitting on the ground near a stream; strafing runs by both Sea Harriers destroyed it. The other two Pumas had also attempted to avoid detection by landing, but after a short cat-and-mouse game, Leeming spotted one of them and Morgan – the only one with any cannon

LEFT A shot-up Argentine Aermacchi MB-339, a trainer type used for light ground-attack duties flying out of Stanley airport. *(Andy Cole)*

ammunition left – critically damaged it with a short burst. The Sea Harriers now had to depart because of low fuel, leaving the very fortunate third Puma free to flee the area, the crew lucky to be alive. Many other Argentine helicopters fell foul of predatory Sea Harriers or GR.3s. Indeed anything with rotors or propellers was particularly vulnerable to the British jets; other kills include Pucarás and, on 1 June, a C-130E brought down over Pebble Island.

Casualties

The narrative above could almost give the impression of a risk-free environment for the British jets, given their total success in air-to-air encounters. In reality, nothing could be further from the truth. In total, six Sea Harriers and three GR.3s were destroyed during the war. Ground fire from radar-controlled cannon plus Argentine SAM systems were the biggest threats. The first aircraft destroyed by AA fire was a Sea Harrier of No. 800 NAS from *Hermes*, shot down by radar-controlled 35mm fire over Goose Green on 4 May. On 21 May and 27 May, No. 1(F) Squadron RAF lost two GR.3s, the first over Port Howard to a Blowpipe SAM and the second once again to 35mm Oerlikon fire over Goose Green, which was proving a very dangerous section of airspace. The squadron took another battle casualty on 30 May, when a Harrier was damaged by small-arms fire from Argentine ground troops, precipitating fuel loss that meant the aircraft was unable to reach *Hermes*; the pilot was forced to eject, and was later picked up. The final kill on a British jet came on 1 June, when a Sea Harrier of No. 801 NAS was brought down by a Roland SAM south of Stanley.

Yet, as is always the case in a busy and complicated combat environment, especially one characterised by such a severe and unpredictable climate, accidental losses were also a major cause of British Sea Harrier/Harrier casualties. The worst of such incidents occurred on 6 May, when two Sea Harriers were destroyed in bad weather, likely because they flew into one another in low visibility. Other losses were taken because of altimeter faults, pilot error, ground crew error and simple unfortunate accidents. On 29 May, for example,

ABOVE AND BELOW Twin 20mm (above) and 35mm (below) Oerlikon cannon, two of the most effective tools of the Argentine air defence. *(Andy Cole)*

a Sea Harrier on *Invincible* was effectively blown off the deck into the sea as the carrier turned into the wind off East Falkland.

Yet as we broaden our analysis away from fixed-wing aircraft, it becomes immediately apparent that one of the most dangerous combat air roles during the Falklands conflict was to be helicopter crew. Not including the rotary assets lost aboard *Atlantic Conveyor*, 14 British helicopters were destroyed during the Falklands War. The reasons behind this higher rate of loss are fairly easy to grasp. Even with the advantages of their terrain-hugging profile, helicopters still fly relatively 'low and slow', making them far easier to target by ground fire. The multi-purpose functions of helicopters also mean that they tend to be used around the clock in all manner of severe weather; the human urgency in CASEVAC missions, or the covert demands of SF insertion/extraction, often means that helicopters fly in weather conditions that would ground most other types. For example, the first two helicopters lost in the war were two Wessex HU.5s of C Flight, No. 845 NAS, which crashed on Fortuna Glacier, South Georgia, while deploying or attempting to extract SAS teams. The most tragic incident, however, occurred on 19 May, when a Sea King HC.4 from *Hermes*, cross-decking an SAS team to *Intrepid*, crashed in the sea following a bird strike; 22 people were killed, including 18 SAS soldiers. In one later incident, on 6 June, a Gazelle of 656 AAC Squadron suffered from a case of mistaken identity when it was shot down over Fitzroy by a Sea Dart fired from HMS *Cardiff*, killing the two crewmen and two men from the Royal Signals. For helicopter crews in particular, even when the levels of Argentine air attacks trailed off during the latter part of the campaign, operational flying remained extremely perilous.

Ground attack

Both fixed-wing jets and helicopters participated in ground-attack roles, onshore and offshore. Offshore, naval helicopters and Sea Harriers from *Hermes* interdicted and sunk or damaged several Argentine vessels, including an early victory against the Argentine submarine *Santa Fe*. On 25 April at South Georgia, a Wessex HAS.3 helicopter from *Antrim* made a radar detection of the Argentine Balao-class submarine *Santa Fe*, which had just successfully dropped off marine reinforcements on the island. The Wessex immediately attacked using its depth charges, catching the *Santa Fe* on the surface, and inflicted serious damage to the craft, including fracturing its ballast tank. Now unable to dive, *Santa Fe* began to struggle back towards Grytviken, but quickly it was under the combined assault of *Antrim*'s Wessex, a Wasp from *Plymouth*, a Lynx from *Brilliant* and further Wasps from *Endurance*. Together the helicopters subjected the submarine to a brutal assault, including multiple AS.12 missiles fired from the Wasps, some of which struck home, and GPMG fire from the Wessex. The submarine

BELOW Snapped by Marine Andy Cole, Chinook 'Bravo November' flies over the San Carlos beachhead, performing a logistical airlift. *(Andy Cole)*

just managed to limp up to the jetty at King Edward Point before being abandoned there in shallow water, the crew leaving the vessel and surrendering to British forces.

Later in the campaign, helicopters also participated in the sinking of the transport *Rio Carcaraña* on 23 May, previously damaged by Sea Harrier attacks but finished off by Sea Skua missiles from a Lynx from HMS *Antelope*, and the damaging of the patrol vessel *Alférez Sobral*. Sea Harriers also unleashed devastation on any Argentine ships they came across, damaging two transport ships (*Bahía Buen Suceso* and *Rio Carcaraña*) and one patrol ship (*Rio Iguazú*), and sinking the trawler *Narwhal* – on 9 May the latter was hit with a 1,000lb (454kg) bomb that failed to explode, then strafed heavily with 30mm cannon fire.

Over ground, we have already seen how Sea Harriers performed ground-attack missions against BAM Malvinas, in the wake of the first Black Buck mission. Both Sea Harriers and GR.3s made low-level combat runs over the air base on several occasions, principally in an attempt to wreck the runway with 1,000lb bombs. As proved to be the case, this was not a simple matter, runways being difficult structures on which to inflict damage that cannot be restored in a few hours by a diligent repair team. Furthermore, the extensive air defences around Stanley meant that these attacks were lethally dangerous, especially from cannon and heavy machine-gun fire. For example, a GR.3 was hit by Oerlikon fire while making a second run across the BAM Malvinas air base, strafing the facilities with ADEN cannon. The hits resulted in a serious and spreading fire, and the pilot (Bob Iveson) was ultimately forced to eject behind enemy lines, although he managed to

RIGHT Night-vision goggles were in limited supply to helicopter pilots during the Falklands conflict, generally being given to those crews involved in SF night deployments.
(Defence Picture Library)

ABOVE A 3 Cdo Bde Air Squadron Scout fitted with SS.11 guided missiles, as used in the Falklands for anti-ship missions. *(Bye for now/ CC BY-SA 4.0)*

2 Para attack against Goose Green and Darwin. The Paras were facing heavy punishment from an Argentine 35mm AA cannon, its barrel depressed to enable it to fire against ground targets. Three Harriers went in low and fast, pounding the AA gun plus the surrounding Argentine positions with CBUs plus a large number of 2in rockets. The Oerlikon was destroyed, and the Harrier assaults softened up the Argentine troops for an advance by 2 Para. Similar attacks were made on Mount Kent the next day, and later upon the various Argentine positions on East Falkland around Stanley.

The use of LGBs, theoretically of the greatest utility against fixed positions, had a somewhat problematic application in the Falklands. The systems in themselves were often not at fault, although bad weather could interfere with the laser designation. Often the more serious problem was the lack of a Forward Air Observer (FAO) to perform the designation, thus on several occasions aircraft returned from their sorties with the bombs still on their racks. The first time they were actually used successfully was on 13 June, in support of British assaults on Mount Tumbledown, when the Harriers had full liaison with an experienced FAO. During the first attack, Harrier XZ997 destroyed an Argentine company HQ with its second LGB (the first fell short). On the same day, another Harrier LGB attack demolished an enemy 105mm gun emplacement at Moody Brook.

stay out of enemy hands and was rescued by a Gazelle three days later.

The arrival of the GR.3s in theatre meant that many of the ground-attack roles performed by the Sea Harriers were transferred to the RAF aircraft. Much of the early ground-attack effort was expended on Argentine positions around Darwin and Goose Green, positions that offered levels of anti-aircraft defence similar to those around Stanley. The Harriers often operated in direct support of British troops, conducting suppression missions against Argentine positions using Cluster Bomb Units (CBUs), rocket pods and even, on occasions, Paveway PGMs. A good example of the Harriers in this role occurred on 28 May in support of the

RIGHT Both the Navy and the RAF deployed Sea King helicopters to the Falklands; their logistical capability earned them the nickname 'Land Rover of the Skies'. *(Defence Picture Library)*

Defining contribution

As stated at the beginning of this chapter, the British air units deployed during the Falklands War were too limited in number to achieve total air superiority over the contested islands. Yet by the end of the war, the Argentine air activity dropped to almost nothing meaningful, at least in terms of fast-jet interventions from the Argentine mainland. By the beginning of June it was clear that, on balance, the British had won the air war.

This victory was not due, to large degree, to any critical disparity between the two sides. The Argentine air forces were, by and large, professional, motivated and flew good aircraft. In February 2013 a British Operational Research Branch review stated as much, in a report declassified and released to the public:

ABOVE The flight deck of HMS *Hermes* in the South Atlantic in early June 1982 with a Harrier GR.3 in the foreground and two Sidewinder-armed Sea Harrier FRS.1s of 800 Naval Air Squadron. *(Crown Copyright)*

The Argentine air arms conducted a 10-week campaign during which time they carried out air supply of their forces in the Falkland Islands, reconnaissance of UK forces in the South Atlantic, and engaged units of TF317. Though they sustained considerable damage, it is fair to say that their air forces were not beaten and remained as a viable force at the end of hostilities. The 4 air arms were, within their own spheres, generally capable and well organised, though limited in AAR and reconnaissance assets. A lack of aircraft spares may also have limited their effectiveness. Of the 3 facets of operations, the Argentine air arms are considered to have been successful in the air supply of their forces, only partially successful in the reconnaissance task, and to have inflicted significant attrition on UK naval forces. No militarily significant success was achieved against UK land forces ashore.[4]

In many ways, the air war was a finely balanced affair that, as the report above hints, turned on a few critical factors, particularly on the issues of range (made problematic by the lack of AAR) and reconnaissance assets. It pushes us to consider how much the outcome of the air war might have been different had the Argentine jets been able to

run at full performance at all times, and had they been able to loiter longer over the target.

Yet this does not take away from the fact that, time and time again, the Argentine aircraft were outflown and outfought, by superbly trained pilots and by excellent and versatile airframes. We can certainly say that without the presence of small numbers of Sea Harriers and Harriers, plus large numbers of rotary assets, the Falklands War could not have been fought.

BELOW Four SAS troopers parachute down to HMS *Cardiff* (into the sea close by) from a C-130 Hercules. *(Ken Griffiths/PD-self)*

Chapter Four

Naval operations

◖─────◉───────────────◗

For the Falklands campaign, the Royal Navy deployed vessels from five general categories of warfighting vessel: submarines, carriers, frigates, destroyers and assault/amphibious ships. The fleet that was eventually assembled was prodigious in scale and firepower. It included two carriers, six submarines, eight destroyers and 15 frigates. When the orders came to form a Task Force, the fleet resources were widely scattered about the UK and abroad. As it turned out, this situation partly worked to the British advantage.

OPPOSITE HMS *Invincible* with a complement of Sea Harriers from No. 801 NAS on the rear deck. *(Defence Picture Library)*

The Royal Navy's 1st Flotilla, 16 warships strong, was at the beginning of April 1982 conducting annual exercises off Gibraltar. Rear Admiral Woodward was the flotilla commander, with the County-class destroyer *Antrim* as his flagship. The advantage lay in the fact that the warships could make preparations for the campaign at Gibraltar itself, instead of sailing home to the UK, and the journey time from Gibraltar to the Falkland Islands was actually three days shorter than the journey vessels would have to make from the UK.

As with the assembly of all war fleets, the Royal Navy component of the Task Force was designed to provide an optimal blend of offensive and defensive capabilities. The submarines offered both anti-ship and anti-submarine services, plus the added advantages of a covert presence, ideal for surveillance and, when required, the deployment of amphibious SF teams. The carriers, the heart of the Task

Force, threw an air-defence umbrella over both the shipping and over the British forces on land, as well as being home to many of the logistical, aerial assault and CASEVAC resources provided by rotary-wing aircraft. (Most of the RN vessels deployed to the Falklands were, to some degree, helicopter enabled.) The numerous frigates and destroyers, allowing for the inevitable overlap between theoretical roles, were primarily used for Task Force missile air defence – working to protect the vital carriers and amphibious assault craft – but also provided ASW, patrol duties and off-shore NGS. Finally, the assault/amphibious vessels had that most critical role in the Falklands campaign, ferrying troops ashore to establish a beachhead, without which the Falklands would have remained permanently in the hands of the Argentines.

In this chapter, we will first unpack the nature of the combat fleet that the Royal Navy deployed to the Falklands, assessing each

BELOW Because HMS *Fearless* was fitted with modern satellite communications equipment it was often used as a command vessel for senior land forces commanders. (*Defence Picture Library*)

type's performance, combat systems, strengths and inevitable weaknesses. With this analysis complete, we then proceed to examine some of the naval actions fought around the Falklands. Here we will run up against the sobering fact that the Royal Navy took losses that, had the conflict played out for any longer than it did, would ultimately have been unsustainable.

Submarines

As noted in a previous chapter, the first ships to sail to the South Atlantic were submarines, and over the weeks of the conflict the total deployment consisted of:

- HMS *Conqueror*
- HMS *Courageous*
- HMS *Spartan*
- HMS *Splendid*
- HMS *Valiant*
- HMS *Onyx*

Most of these, with the exception of the diesel-electric powered *Onyx*, were nuclear-powered hunter/attack submarines, intended not for delivering Polaris nuclear missile strikes – such was never a considered option for the Falklands Task Force – but for anti-ship and ASW roles. Nuclear-powered vessels (SSNs) had a natural value for the Falklands deployment, their powerplants offering almost unlimited running time, without the need for refuelling, which gave them enormous range and both surfaced and submerged endurance. The nuclear vessels were faster both on the surface and below; for example, *Conqueror* had a submerged speed of 28 knots (52km/h), while *Onyx* was limited to 17 knots (31km/h). The engines also ran far quieter than diesel-electrics, a crucial factor considering that auditory detection was a key technology in ASW, plus they did not need to resurface periodically to maintain the running of the engines. By contrast, the diesel-electric submarines (SSKs) were obliged either to surface intermittently or to 'snorkel' (extend an air intake mast above the surface of the water) to power the air-breathing diesel engines; running the diesel engines was required to recharge the electric batteries aboard the ship. Taking on air was a vulnerable moment for an

SSK, as breaking the surface made the vessel more exposed to radar detection. For the SSN, the main reason it was compelled to surface was to take on food and supplies, but given that its internal stocks could last months, they were largely hidden warriors. The main advantage of the SSKs, however, was their generally lower displacement, which meant that they could deploy into shallow coastal areas inaccessible to their nuclear-powered cousins; thus *Onyx* was used to deploy SBS units ashore.

The SSNs and SSKs detected enemy submarines or surface vessels through a mix of radar and active and passive sonar arrays. *Conqueror*, for example, was fitted with the Kelvin Type 1008 surface-search radar and the Type 2020 sonar array and a Type 2026 towed array – the latter was towed behind the submarine for distances up to a mile, to improve the clarity of detecting submerged and surface vessels.

The primary weapon system of the submarines was their torpedoes, which at the time consisted of two main types. The most advanced was the Mk 24 Tigerfish, an acoustic homing torpedo fitted with wire guidance to allow onboard directional control to target. It could be used against submarines (the torpedo had a crush depth of 2,000ft (610m) and

ABOVE Five Sub-Surface Nuclear (SSNs) and one diesel-powered submarine deployed to the Falklands. HMS *Conqueror* spearheaded the first naval strike – sinking the Argentine light cruiser *General Belgrano*. *(Defence Picture Library)*

against surface targets, and had a maximum firing range of 24 miles (39km). It did, however, garner a reputation for unreliability, either in failing to detonate the warhead at the target or in losing command control, particularly at range. Less sophisticated, but more reliable, were the Mk VIII torpedoes, which had an ancestry dating back to the 1920s. These were straight-running, unguided torpedoes, with a maximum range of around 4 miles (6.5km), but they at least had a proven performance, which was probably a critical factor in their use by *Conqueror* against the *General Belgrano*, in preference to the advanced Tigerfish.

The submarines' torpedoes were typically supplemented by the UGM-84 Harpoon all-weather, over-the-horizon, anti-ship missile system. These missiles could be launched from a submerged position, and once above the water they would adopt a sea-skimming flight profile to the target, using active radar homing to guide it to targets more than 37 miles (60km) away.

Carriers

The development of Britain's post-war carriers is a convoluted story, both from technological and political perspectives, and cannot be told in full here. In rough outline, during the 1960s the MOD decided that full-scale aircraft carriers, deploying large squadrons of fixed-wing, conventional take-off aircraft were no longer relevant to the modern age or to the strained British purse. It was therefore decided that replacement carriers would not be built when the three carriers in service came to be decommissioned. Instead, the Royal Navy would focus on smaller vessels equipped with missile-armed helicopters for anti-ship, ASW and assault roles, and also (when required/feasible) units of Sea Harrier V/STOL aircraft, which could provide air interception and CAS missions. In appearance, these vessels looked like aircraft carriers, but to avoid the politics of that label they were named 'Through-deck cruisers', although the term was fooling no one, least of all the Navy. To most, and to posterity, they are still known as aircraft carriers.

At the time of the Falklands, there were three carriers in British service: the Centaur-class HMS *Hermes* (commissioned 1959) and HMS *Bulwark* (1954), and the far more modern HMS *Invincible*, the lead ship of her class (1980). These resources, already stretched for conducting a major expeditionary conflict, were tightened even further by a ship survey of *Bulwark* when the conflict began, which found that the vessel's material and systems deterioration made it unfit for service in the conflict.

Hermes was the larger of the two carriers, at 28,000 tonnes full load displacement. For more than a decade, *Hermes* was a classic fixed-wing aircraft carrier, deploying Buccaneers, Sea Vixens and Gannets, plus Sea King helicopters. During the 1960s and '70s, however, she was variously redesignated as a Commando/ASW/

STOVL carrier, undergoing some significant physical modifications in the process. Most important – especially in the context of the Falklands War – was the fitting of a 12-degree 'ski-jump' on the flight deck at the beginning of the 1980s. This system enabled the Sea Harriers to take off from a forward roll, rather than via the highly fuel-consuming vertical take-off, by converting some of the forward motion into a positive rate of climb. It was a successful system, also fitted to *Invincible*, and its adoption would have great significance for the success of British air operations in the Falklands. Air-defence armament consisted of ten 40mm Bofors guns plus two Seacat missile launchers.

Invincible was a smaller (displacement: 22,000 tonnes fully loaded) but more modern carrier, powered by four Rolls-Royce Olympus TM3B Marine gas turbines (at that time she was the largest ship in the world to run on gas turbines). Listed air complement was five Sea

BELOW Helicopter ops aboard HMS *Invincible*. Of note on the flight deck is the Bv 206 tracked articulated all-terrain vehicle in the foreground. *(Defence Picture Library)*

HMS *HERMES* SPECIFICATIONS

Class and type:	Centaur-class aircraft carrier
Displacement:	23,000 tonnes standard; 28,000 tonnes full load
Length:	744ft 5in (226.9m) overall (with ski-jump)
Beam:	144ft (43.9m) flight deck
Draught:	27ft 11in (8.5m)
Propulsion:	2 × Parsons SR geared turbines, 76,000shp (57 MW); 4 × Admiralty 3-drum boilers
Speed:	28 knots (32mph; 52km/h)
Range:	7,000nmi (13,000km) at 18kn (20.5mph; 33km/h)
Complement:	2,100
Armament:	10 × 40mm Bofors; 2 × Seacat launchers
Aircraft carried:	Up to 28 Sea Harriers and 9 Westland Sea Kings (theoretical)

Harriers and nine Sea Kings, the weighting towards ASW-capable helicopters indicating the carrier's official status as an 'ASW carrier'. Just prior to the Falklands War, *Invincible* was actually intended for sale to the Australian Navy in 1983, the transfer meant to occur as *Invincible*'s sister ship *Illustrious*, then being built, came into service. Only the Falklands War reversed this decision.

Invincible was a sophisticated vessel, replete with modern surveillance, navigation and fire-control radar, the latter for the twin Seacat launchers on board. Yet like *Hermes*, during the Falklands War *Invincible*'s main instrument of offence and defence was its air complement of ASW helicopters and Sea Harriers.

The value of the carriers for the Falklands campaign was inestimable, and arguably the war could not have been fought at all without their presence. Yet the Task Force was not carrier-strong in the same way as a US Navy CVBG. Indeed, a US analysis shortly after the war laid bare what it saw as the key deficiencies of these two vessels:

> *The smaller carriers are far less sustainable. Propelled by gas turbines or, in the case of HERMES, steam turbines, these ships have relatively limited endurance before they require refueling. They also have limited on-board stowage for ordnance. In the Falklands, both ships had flight decks encumbered by stacks of bombs, missiles, and fuel tanks which could not be fitted into the ships' magazines, thus making them very vulnerable had any Argentine aircraft been able to locate and attack them. In contrast, nuclear-powered U.S. carriers not only have virtually unlimited steaming endurance, they also carry thousands of tons of munitions and months' worth of spare parts for all of their embarked aircraft. Additionally, our carriers have extensive on-board repair facilities which cannot be provided on a small carrier. Taken together, two British carriers were able to operate less than 30 V/STOL aircraft and about a dozen ASW helicopters at the peak intensity of combat activity. That's about 50,000 tons of aircraft carriers to operate one-third of the number of far more capable aircraft that we carry in one 90,000-ton NIMITZ class carrier.*[1]

The comparison is, on one level, unreflective on actual vs optimum requirements, but it does make some valuable points about the vulnerabilities and limitations of British carrier forces in the Falklands. Had Britain been able to deploy more carriers, with large numbers of fixed-wing air assets, the attrition of Task Force shipping to Argentine air attacks might have been considerably reduced.

Destroyers

If the carriers were the heart of the Task Force, then the destroyers and frigates were the protective ribs and skin around it. The classic role of the destroyer has been to provide escort to and defence for larger vessels against short-range attacks. By the time of the Falklands War, a destroyer's purpose primarily revolved around air defence through onboard short- and medium-range SAM systems, plus the ability to engage enemy surface vessels with anti-ship missiles – either fired from the ship or launched from one of the vessel's armed helicopters – or submarines through one of its ASW systems. The presence of a forward-mounted gun, moreover, meant that destroyers could also provide NGS against land targets within the range of the shell.

Three classes of destroyer were taken to the Falklands:

Type	Ship	Displacement	Weapon systems
Type 82	*Bristol*	6,400 tonnes standard	Sea Dart SAM Ikara ASW missile system 1 × 4.5in Mk 8 gun Mk 10 Anti-Submarine Mortar 1 × Wasp helicopter
County class	*Antrim* *Glamorgan*	6,200 tonnes standard	Exocet SSM Seaslug/Seacat SAM STWS anti-submarine torpedo launchers 2 × 4.5in Mk 6 (twin turret) 2 × Oerlikon 20mm cannon 1 × Wessex HAS Mk 3 helicopter
Type 42	*Cardiff* *Coventry* *Exeter* *Glasgow* *Sheffield*	4,100 tonnes standard	Sea Dart SAM STWS anti-submarine torpedo launchers 1 × 4.5in Mk 8 gun 2 × Oerlikon 20mm cannon 1 × Westland Lynx

BELOW Owing to some design shortcuts, the seakeeping of the Type 42 left a lot to be desired; they were known to be punishing on the crew above and below decks. *(Defence Picture Library)*

The largest of these types, *Bristol*, was in fact the only ship of its class. It was commissioned in 1973, and originally conceived as an escort for large carriers, but the 1966 decision to scrap aircraft carriers meant that only one of the class was actually built, and primarily as a testbed for various warfare systems. The oldest of the destroyers were the County class; *Glamorgan* had been commissioned in 1966 and *Antrim* in 1970, two of eight County-class ships laid down between 1959 and 1966. The County class was specifically a guided-missile destroyer – the first such vessels in the Royal Navy – its armament stacked towards guided missile systems for engaging ships, aircraft and submarines.

Yet the most numerous of the destroyers were the Type 42s (or *Sheffield* class), 14 of which had been built for the Royal Navy by the time of the Falklands War, the first (*Sheffield*) being commissioned into service in 1975. Like the County-class ships, the Type 42s were primarily intended for the missile-armed air defence and anti-ship/submarine roles. Under the hard economic conditions of the 1960s and '70s, however, they were built with budget restrictions firmly in mind, their numbers meant to offset the cancellation of most of the Type 82 destroyers. Their status as 'austerity destroyers' was evident in many of the design details. The hull length was shorter than advisable, resulting in poor seakeeping characteristics that not only affected the health, morale and efficiency of the crew, but also had an impact on operating deck-mounted systems, particularly the forward gun and SAM launchers. Furthermore, the short hull resulted in cramped interior operating spaces, particularly regarding the operations room; staff operating the ship's complex defence systems sometimes struggled simply to move around the command space. On the plus side, the Type 42s were fast boats, achieving up to 30 knots (35mph; 56km/h), albeit at the cost of heavy fuel consumption.

Frigates

The Royal Navy deployed 16 frigates down to the Falklands, making them the most numerous of the combat vessels. Frigates, at this stage in maritime history, were theoretically focused upon the role of ASW, although their deployment of SAM systems meant that at the Falklands they, along with the destroyers, formed an integral part of the air-defence screen thrown around the Task Force.

The frigates sent to the Falklands were:

Type	Ship	Displacement	Typical weapon systems
Type 22	*Brilliant* *Broadsword*	4,400–4,800 tonnes standard	Exocet SSM Sea Wolf SAM STWS anti-submarine torpedo launchers 2 × 40mm Bofors 2 × Lynx helicopters
Type 21	*Active* *Alacrity* *Ambuscade* *Antelope* *Ardent* *Arrow* *Avenger*	2,860 tonnes standard	Exocet SSM Seacat SAM STWS anti-submarine torpedo launchers 2 × 20mm Oerlikon cannon 1 × 4.5in gun 1 × Wasp or Lynx helicopter
Leander class	*Andromeda* *Argonaut* *Minerva* *Penelope*	2,790 tonnes standard	Exocet SSM or 2 × 4.5in Mk 6 guns (twin turret) Sea Wolf or Seacat SAM STWS anti-submarine torpedo launchers 4 × 20mm cannon 1 × Lynx helicopter
Rothesay class	*Plymouth* *Yarmouth*	2,180 tonnes standard	2 × 4.5in Mk 6 guns (twin turret) Seacat SAM 1 × Limbo ASW mortar 2 × 20mm cannon 1 × Wasp helicopter

The frigates deployed as part of the Task Force gave the fleet a dense SAM screen, on which it would rely heavily during the battles around the Falkland Islands in May 1982. As is evident from the list above, and that of the destroyers, the Seacat and Sea Wolf systems dominated, so it is worth describing them in a little more detail.

The Seacat was a point-defence system developed by the UK Short Brothers company and introduced into service in 1962. It developed as a replacement for the shipborne 40mm Bofors cannon (although many of those guns stayed in service), for engaging proximate aircraft threats from ranges of 547–5,468yd (500–5,000m). It was actually in many ways a

SAM spin-off of the Malkara anti-tank missile, and also used command line-of-sight (CLOS) guidance via a radio link, which meant that the observer had to keep in his sights the target aircraft and missile, flying the latter on to the former. This was the Guided Weapon System 20 (GWS) used aboard most of the ships, although the County-class destroyers had the updated GWS-21, which had radar-assisted guidance and tracking options. Flight speed was subsonic.

The Sea Dart system offered greater range in the SAM umbrella – 30 nautical miles (35 miles; 56km) – with a missile flying at supersonic speeds for rapid interceptions. Guidance was by proportional navigation and semi-active radar homing, but operational use in the Falklands showed that while the system performed decently at medium to long ranges, at close ranges it struggled to acquire and hit the target. Sea Wolf, by contrast, was ostensibly ideal for shorter range point defence, being a more modern system than the Seacat. In fact, Sea Wolf was largely designed as an SSM interception missile, but also provided close air defence in the 1,093–6,561yd (1,000–6,000m) ranges. The importance of the system was its fully automated radar tracking guidance system, which enabled missile firing even without human intervention, although the Type 910 guidance system in use at the time did feature

ABOVE A Royal Navy 40mm Bofors installation. In some warships, AA cannon had been replaced by point-defence SAM systems, although as it turned out AA gunnery remained one of the most effective measures against low-level jet attack. *(Defence Picture Library)*

ABOVE RIGHT Leander-class frigate HMS *Phoebe*, which deployed to the Falklands in September 1982. Note how the forward 4.5in gun has been replaced by Exocet anti-ship missile launchers. *(Defence Picture Library)*

BELOW The ARA *General Belgrano* was previously the USS *Phoenix*, a Second World War vintage light cruiser, in service with the Argentine Navy from 1951. *(Defence Picture Library)*

a secondary TV mode for manual tracking to target.

It would be these three systems, accompanied by rippling banks of traditional AA fire from cannon and machine guns, which would be tested in one of the most demanding combat environments possible around the Falklands in 1982. (See below for further performance analysis.)

Sinking the *General Belgrano*

One of the key events that turned the Falklands invasion from a diplomatic game of brinkmanship into a full-blown shooting war came on 2 May 1982, with the sinking of the Argentine cruiser ARA *General Belgrano*. By this time, the UK armed forces had declared two exclusion zones around the Falklands. The first, known as the Maritime Exclusion Zone (MEZ), was established on 12 April 1982, an area defined by a circle extending 200 nautical miles (230 miles; 370km) out from the centre of the Falkland Islands. The MEZ declaration stated that any Argentine warship or naval auxiliary entering the MEZ could be attacked by British SSNs. The Total Exclusion Zone (TEZ) of 30 April kept the same area of prohibition, but widened the

rules of engagement. A passage from the official communiqué delivered to the Swiss Embassy in Buenos Aires on 23 April stated that:

Her Majesty's Government now wishes to make clear that any approach on the part of Argentine warships, including submarines, naval auxiliaries or military aircraft, which could amount to a threat to interfere with the mission of British Forces in the South Atlantic will encounter the appropriate response. All Argentine aircraft, including civil aircraft engaged in surveillance of these British forces, will be regarded as hostile and are liable to be dealt with accordingly.

As this statement made clear, from this point on any Argentine object, flying or floating, entering the TEZ was now open to being attacked and destroyed.

On 26 April, the ARA *General Belgrano* set sail from Ushuaia, in the far southern tip of Argentina, and headed for the Falklands Islands. Together with two destroyers, *Hipólito Buchard* and *Piedra Buena*, it formed Task Group 79.3, part of the Task Group 79 which potentially appeared to be trapping the British fleet in a pincer movement. Bearing down from the north were Task Groups 79.1, 79.2 and 79.4, which between them included the Skyhawk-laden carrier *Veinticinco de Mayo*, two destroyers, three frigates and a submarine. The British Task Force relayed information about the enemy vessels back to London, and waited for a decision. Margaret Thatcher's cabinet, plus the staff at Northwood, agonised over what to do, principally in the case of the *General Belgrano*, which although still outside the TEZ was closing up its distance with the Task Force. Leave it be, and it could attack British shipping; sink it, and it would likely result in a very heavy loss of life (the cruiser had a complement of 1,000 men) and a profound escalation in the military option. Yet the decision had to be made quickly. *Belgrano* was being tracked by HMS *Conqueror*, and *Conqueror*'s commander, Commander Chris Wreford-Brown, feared that it might be lost to the British when it entered the approaching Burdwood Bank, where the water was too shallow for the submarine to operate. The order came through – sink the *Belgrano*.

Even though it was still outside the TEZ, it was only six hours away from the Task Force (35 miles/56km outside the TEZ) and represented a clear threat.

At 16:00hrs (local time), *Conqueror* fired a spread of three Mk 8 torpedoes, from a distance of 3 miles (5km), the Mk 8s offering more rapid deployment and greater reliability than the Mk 24 torpedoes. Two of the torpedoes struck home, the first hitting the ship on the port bow and the second striking near the stern, around the after machinery room. Both exploded properly, with a truly devastating effect on the ageing cruiser. The whole front of the bow collapsed and the engines went dead. Hundreds of men died in just those first few minutes, either from the explosions or from being trapped in some of the rear spaces as thousands of tons of South Atlantic seawater rushed in. Secondary explosions followed, the response to which was hampered by the fact that about 30% of the crew were teenage recruits, unversed in emergency response procedures. But soon any attempt to save the ship was futile – within ten minutes she was at a 15-degree list, and within 60 minutes she had capsized and sunk. About 650 men went into the sea in lifeboats, most – not all – to be rescued later in treacherous and freezing seas. But around 368 of the crew members died, a chilling figure both to the Argentines but also to the British, who realised that the opportunity for

ABOVE ARA *General Belgrano* **sinks after being struck by two Mk 8 torpedoes fired from HMS** *Conqueror*. *(Defence Picture Library)*

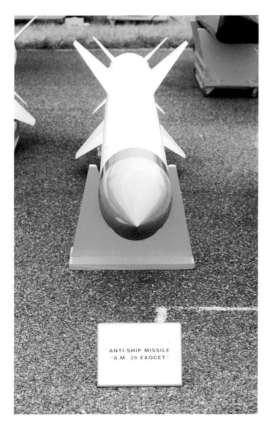

ANTI-SHIP MISSILE
"A.M. 39 EXOCET"

diplomacy was largely gone now, and that the Argentines would be keen to exact retribution. Two armed tugs on a rescue mission, *Alférez Sobral* and *Comodoro Somellera*, were later shot up by British helicopters when they opened fire on the helicopters with a heavy machine gun.

The Exocet onslaught

It is a by-product of major conflicts that publicly little-known weapon systems sometimes became household names on the back of their notoriety. The Exocet anti-ship missile is a case in point. The destructive efficiency of this missile in the Falklands, expressed most visibly in its sinking of HMS *Sheffield* and the *Atlantic Conveyor*, made it a much-feared element of the Argentine arsenal.

On the afternoon of 4 May, HMS *Sheffield*, commanded by Captain James 'Sam' Salt, was deployed within the TEZ, the most southerly of three Type 42 destroyers responsible for the Task Force air-defence screen, 18 miles (29km) to the west of the main body of ships. The ship's company was in Defence Watches and Damage Control State 2, the second level of alertness that allowed the crew to rotate in and out of six-hour watches, some performing their duties while others took the opportunity to eat or sleep.

Shortly before 10:00hrs local time, HMS *Glasgow* detected incoming hostile aircraft at a range of about 40 miles (64km); these were in fact two Super Étendard aircraft equipped with AM.39 Exocets, the aircraft and the missiles together representing the most high-tech Argentine threat to the British Task Force. Unfortunately, *Glasgow*'s report of the raid – identified as the 'racket Condor 245' – was downgraded to a yellow status by its conflicting with signals information from other sources. Yet when they were about 15 miles (24km) from *Sheffield*, the two aircraft swung around on an attack trajectory and launched their Exocets.

At the time of writing this book, a full unredacted report of the sinking of HMS *Sheffield* has been released to the media. (Excerpts from the original redacted report are reprinted here.) It has revealed some telling facts about the moments leading to the impact upon the ship. Most critically, it had to address why the ship: a) did not detect the attacks itself, and engage either the aircraft or the missiles with Sea Dart or 4.5in gun; or b) did not employ basic defensive responses, such as turning the bows towards the missiles (to present a smaller target) or firing chaff to interfere with the missile tracking system. The recent revelations have uncovered some additional elements to existing public knowledge:

■ The lower level of readiness had resulted in the anti-air warfare officer leaving the room at crucial moments to get a cup of coffee; his assistant was also absent, having gone to the toilet.

■ The principal warfare officer failed to respond to the reports from *Glasgow* 'partly through inexperience, but more importantly from inadequacy'.

■ A call was put out to recall the anti-air warfare officer back to the operations room, but he believed that *Sheffield* was out of range of the Argentine aircraft.

■ Finally, the officers on the bridge became 'mesmerised' by the sight of the missile coming towards them (once they had visual

contact) and failed to broadcast a warning to the crew.[2]

In addition to the above, the ship's Type 966 radar was switched off to prevent interference with the main surveillance radar, plus the ship's Electronic Support Measures (ESM) equipment was suffering from interference from other surface-warning radars in the fleet, which actually broadcast on the same frequency as the Exocet seeker head.

From the safety and comfort of both hindsight and peacetime, we should be very slow to pass judgement on the individuals aboard the *Sheffield*, especially as for most it would likely have been their first time in a combat theatre. Nevertheless, significant errors in defence seem to have been made.

A single Exocet hit *Sheffield* on the starboard side amidships, on Deck 2 level, and ripped open a hole 15ft × 4ft (4.6 × 1.2m) in the side of the ship. According to subsequent analysis, the warhead itself did not explode (the Admiralty report described that there was little evidence of shrapnel), but the impact effects and the burning of unspent fuel resulted in catastrophic fires, which spread with alarming rapidity and

ABOVE Seen through the forward window of a rescue helicopter, HMS *Sheffield* on fire after being hit by an Exocet strike on 4 May 1982. *(Defence Picture Library)*

BELOW Weapon directors plot a navigation map in the operations room of a frigate. The crewmen are wearing anti-flash hoods and gloves to protect them from a 'flash over' caused by an impact of a missile or bomb attack. *(Defence Picture Library)*

EXCERPTS FROM ADMIRALTY REPORT (REDACTED) ON SINKING OF HMS *SHEFFIELD* (JULY 1982)

5. SHEFFIELD's assessment of the threat on 4 May acknowledged the possibility of SUPER E/EXOCET attack, and that such an attack could be at low level. However other types of attack, particularly from submarines, were considered more likely.

[. . .]

10. [REDACTED SECTION] Neither Sea Dart nor 4.5 inch Mk 8 engaged the missile or the firing aircraft. 4.5 inch alarm procedure was not used.

11. [REDACTED SECTION] Weapons were neither manned nor loaded. They were not able to indicate or engage.

[. . .]

14. If all the right reactions had been taken, very quickly indeed, and in particular if Chaff D had been fired on receipt of the CONDOR racket from GLASGOW, it might just have been possible to frustrate this very determined and very professional SUPER E/EXOCET attack.

15. In any such circumstances the provision of longer warning, as from AEW, must enhance the chances of successful defence.

16. Some shortcomings in the Type 42's defence capabilities against such an attack were borne out by the evidence heard. The most important of these are:-

a) Lack of a Jammer.

b) The very high reliance demanded on a number of operators if a Sea Dart or 4.5 inch versus sea skimmer engagement is to have any chance of success.

c) Lack of a Point Defence System.

d) Inadequate simulator provision, particularly for realistic 909 low target acquisition practice.[3]

filled the working spaces of the ship with a thick, poisonous and suffocating smoke. Electrical power failed – the main generator in the after engine room had been destroyed by the missile impact and the forward main generator had been stripped for repair. The ship was progressively becoming a more toxic environment for the crew, and damage-control systems, now without power, were failing to control the fire. With the possibility of the ship's ammunition magazine exploding, Captain Salt eventually gave the order to abandon ship. Twenty-one men had died, and dozens had been seriously injured. *Sheffield* herself managed to stay afloat for another five days, before finally sinking.

The destruction of the *Sheffield* was a shocking demonstration of the power of modern anti-ship missiles, but further terrible instruction was to come. On 25 May, Exocet-armed Super Étendards again scored a brutal triumph, this time against the container ship *Atlantic Conveyor*. The *Atlantic Conveyor*'s material cargo could hardly have been more precious: it included a Lynx helicopter, six Wessex HU5s and three Chinooks (out of four deployed to the theatre), the Chinooks were intended to provide the main helicopter logistical support of the land campaign. Also on board were dozens of air-dropped munitions, a portable airstrip and tents for 4,000 men.

Around 19:30hrs the two Argentine aircraft had unleashed their Exocets towards a mass of

RIGHT HMS *Sheffield* on fire after being hit by an Argentine Exocet missile. Such sinkings caused the Admiralty to make major revisions to its fire-prevention policy.
(Defence Picture Library)

Task Force shipping north-east of the Falklands. Indeed, it might have been the case that the Exocets were fired without a specific target in mind. They appear, however, to have been heading towards *Hermes*, but then changed course and acquired a new target – the *Atlantic Conveyor* – when *Hermes* fired off 'Corvus' chaff rockets to interfere with the Exocets' guidance systems.

Both missiles struck *Atlantic Conveyor*, with devastating results. As with *Sheffield*, fire was quickly raging throughout the ship, resulting in the detonation of stores of fuel and munitions. Twelve men died, including the captain, Ian North, while the remainder of the crew were eventually rescued before the ship broke its back and slipped under the water. It was a loss that changed the very nature of the Falklands campaign for the British.

There would be one final Exocet incident before the end of the war, this occurring on 12 June. By this time, the County-class destroyer *Glamorgan* had already tasted combat, and had been slightly damaged by Argentine bombing on 1 May. On 11 June, she was deployed off Stanley to provide NGS to Royal Marines engaged in the battle of Two Sisters.

It was in this position that *Glamorgan* faced a new threat – two MM38 surface-to-surface Exocets, actually Exocets removed from the ARA *Guerrico* and fitted to ground-launchers.

At 06:37hrs, some 18 miles (29km) offshore, *Glamorgan* was suddenly struck by a single MM38. Air defence radars had acquired the missiles, and thankfully the Officer of the Watch spotted the missiles visually, and was able to turn the ship stern-on before the missile hit. The missile struck the stern, but failed to detonate the warhead. It was still a consequential and dangerous impact, however. Fourteen crew members were killed, and there was a major fire in the helicopter hangar, where a Wessex helicopter was set ablaze. Nevertheless, effective fire-control procedures were put in place, and the fires were out by 10:00hrs.

The Exocet missiles were among the most dangerous assets in the Argentine arsenal, especially for a British Task Force entirely reliant on shipping. It is fortunate that Argentina could not source and deploy more of the missiles in action; a single effective Exocet strike on a carrier could have dramatically changed the war.

Argentine air attacks

Although the Exocets achieved significant damage within the Task Force – sinking two ships and damaging a third – there emerged a far greater danger to British shipping. That accolade goes to conventional bombing attacks delivered at low level, principally by Skyhawk and Mirage aircraft.

ABOVE Photographed in Stanley just after the Argentine surrender, here we see a land-based twin Exocet launcher, a serious threat to RN vessels off the Falklands coast. It would likely have been this launcher that fired the missile that struck HMS *Glamorgan*. *(Andy Cole)*

air attacks of a scale that hadn't been seen since the Second World War. Most of the strikes were fast and low, the jets taking advantage of the coastal contours to emerge suddenly, attack the ships with strafing runs or bomb drops, then disappear over an adjacent bay or nearby hill.

The consequences stunned the world's naval community. During the Falklands War, the British lost seven major vessels, comprising HMS *Sheffield*, HMS *Ardent*, HMS *Antelope*, RFA *Sir Galahad*, HMS *Coventry*, *Atlantic Conveyor* and HMS *Fearless*. Many more were damaged to varying degrees, some so significantly that they had to be removed from the campaign and headed back to Britain. That this occurred in a truly modern Navy with some of the latest air-defence technology made the situation even more concerning.

It is impossible here to provide a full explanation of the battle history of each of the ships that fought in the Falklands. The following table, however, provides a list of the ships damaged and sunk.

ABOVE HMS *Plymouth* smoulders after being hit by four Argentine bombs in San Carlos Water on 8 June. *(Defence Picture Library)*

Throughout May 1982, and into early June, British shipping around the Falklands – particularly when operating in the NGS gunlines off Stanley, or when supporting or delivering the amphibious landings at San Carlos or Fitzroy – was subjected to intensive, prolonged

Date	Ship	Status	Notes
1 May	HMS *Alacrity*	Damaged	Off Stanley; bomb near misses
	HMS *Arrow*	Damaged	Off Stanley; cannon fire damage
	HMS *Glamorgan*	Damaged	Off Stanley; bomb near misses
4 May	HMS *Sheffield*	**Sunk**	South-east of Falklands; Exocet attack
12 May	HMS *Glasgow*	Damaged	Off Stanley; superstructure and hull damaged by UXB; returned to UK
21 May	HMS *Antrim*	Damaged	Falkland Sound outside San Carlos Water; damage from UXB; took several days to remove bomb and repair damage
	HMS *Broadsword*	Damaged	Outside San Carlos Water; cannon-fire damage
	HMS *Argonaut*	Damaged	Outside San Carlos Water; initial damage from rockets and cannon fire, then serious damage from two UXBs
	HMS *Brilliant*	Damaged	Outside San Carlos Water; cannon-fire damage (slight)
	HMS *Ardent*	**Sunk**	Grantham Sound; multiple bomb hits and near misses; sank on 22 May
23 May	HMS *Antelope*	**Sunk**	San Carlos Water; hit by two UXBs; one exploded while being defused; ship sank on 24 May
24 May	RFA *Sir Galahad*	Damaged	San Carlos Water; hit by UXB; out of action for several days
	RFA *Sir Lancelot*	Damaged	San Carlos Water; hit by UXB; out of action for eight days
	RFA *Sir Bedivere*	Damaged	San Carlos Water; slight bomb damage
25 May	HMS *Broadsword*	Damaged	North of Pebble Island; bomb damage
	HMS *Coventry*	**Sunk**	North of Pebble Island; three bomb strikes
	Atlantic Conveyor	**Sunk**	North-east of Falklands, Exocet strikes
29 May	*British Wye*	Damaged	North of South Georgia; slight bomb damage
8 June	HMS *Plymouth*	Damaged	Falkland Sound off San Carlos Water; four UXBs
	RFA *Sir Galahad*	**Sunk**	Off Fitzroy; set on fire by bomb strikes
	RFA *Sir Tristram*	Damaged	Off Fitzroy; bomb strikes; abandoned but later repaired
	HMS *Fearless*	**Sunk**	Choiseul Sound; bomb strike
12 June	HMS *Glamorgan*	Damaged	Off Stanley; land-based Exocet attack

The list, in its brevity, masks a world of tragedy, often played out on TV sets in the living rooms of people around the United Kingdom. The sinking of the RFA *Sir Galahad* on 8 June off Fitzroy represents the greatest single loss of life: 48 soldiers (principally men of the Welsh Guards) and crew died in catastrophic fires after being attacked by three A-4 Skyhawks from the Argentine Air Force's V Brigada Aérea, which hit the vessel with two or three 500lb (227kg) bombs. Yet as the list above shows, even the well-armed modern fighting vessels were also victims to sweeping attacks by the Argentine aircraft. A representative example of such a loss is that of the Type 42 destroyer HMS *Coventry*, commanded by Captain David Hart Dyke.

On 25 May 1982, *Coventry* was deployed around the Amphibious Operating Area, acting as part of the air-defence screen for the two British carriers plus the landing site around San Carlos. Her main contribution to the air-defence duties was to use her Type 965 long-range surveillance radar to vector Sea Harriers to intercept incoming air raids – on 24 May alone *Coventry* assisted in three Sea Harrier kills of Argentine aircraft – while also providing a medium-range SAM screen via her Sea Dart system. (*Coventry* was paired with *Broadsword* in the operating area, the latter complementing *Coventry*'s medium-range SAMs with its short-range Sea Wolf system.) From first light on 25 May, both vessels, and indeed the British fleet in general, came under especially intense

and prolonged air attack. The first Argentine strike was successfully detected and engaged, with Sea Dart used to destroy two incoming jets; within an hour, another attacker had been downed. Following a break in the onslaught around midday, the action then resumed in the early afternoon, the Argentine pilots flying in low over the Falklands land mass to break the defenders' radar contact. Two Skyhawks appeared from over Pebble Island; their appearance was so sudden that it was impossible to deploy the SAM systems, *Coventry* instead engaging with the 4.5in gun, Oerlikon cannon and GPMGs. One aircraft was hit during this pass, but *Broadsword* received a bomb strike that smashed through the quarterdeck and destroyed a helicopter. Captain Hart Dyke, in his later account of *Coventry's* service in the Falklands, noted of this moment:

We had been lucky so far, although it was extremely unfortunate that Broadsword had not been able to engage the aircraft with her Sea Wolf missiles. We learnt later that she had had the pair of Skyhawks clearly in her missile sights but the system would not lock on to either of them and actually switched off at the critical moment. The system's software had a limitation: it could not decide which target to fire at when two aircraft were flying close together and at the same range.[4]

Following this attack, radar signatures indicated that another Argentine run – probably by four aircraft – was coming in, but the on-screen picture was confusing to interpret. A Sea Dart was fired at one of the aircraft, but then two others appeared, coming in so low and fast that they were whipping up the sea behind them. There was no time to engage with the SAMs, and *Broadsword* had her view of the attackers blocked by *Coventry*. Gunners aboard *Coventry* opened up with everything they had, but then the Oerlikon jammed, leaving a crucial gap through which the two Skyhawks flew and released their bombs. Hart Dyke explains the trauma of the subsequent events:

BELOW The Type 42 destroyer HMS *Coventry* lying on her port side before she sank in 300ft (91m) of water, 13 miles (21km) north of Pebble Island, West Falkland. *(Defence Picture Library)*

The sinister silence in Coventry *was abruptly shattered by two 1,000-pound bombs exploding. In the operations room there was a vicious shockwave, a blinding flash and searing heat. I felt as though I had been caught in a doorway and a heavy door had been slammed against me: the force and the shock of the impact shook my whole body to the core. I was stunned into unconsciousness. When I came to my senses, I was still sitting, very precariously, on the edge of my now broken chair in front of the radar screen into which I had been peering intently a few seconds before. But the screen was no longer there: it had simply disintegrated. [. . .] I looked to my left and saw a sheet of flame leap out of the hatch down into the computer room below and envelop a man as he attempted to climb into the operations room. He had nearly reached the top of the ladder, and someone had stretched towards him and tried to catch his hand. But it was too late: consumed by fire, he could go no further and fell back with a final, despairing cry for help. In the hellish furnace that the computer room had become were seven key members of the weapons engineering department, among them Lieutenant Rod Heath, their leader. The blast of the bomb would have killed the majority of them outright.*[5]

Hart Dyke's harrowing and compelling account of these destructive moments confronts us with the appalling human consequences of modern air-dropped munitions. *Coventry* rapidly began to list and Hart Dyke promptly gave the order to abandon ship; within 15 minutes the ship had capsized. In total, 19 crew were killed in the attack.

Some points emerge from this assault, and other similar raids on the British fleet. The first is that in some ways *Coventry* was unlucky that both of the Argentine bombs exploded. In 13 instances during the war, mercifully, Argentine bombs struck British ships but were released at too low an altitude to fuse properly, therefore not exploding. It is for this reason that Lord Craig, retired Marshal of the RAF, remarked with chilling hindsight 'six better fuses and we would have lost'. The other key lesson of the Task Force naval battle against the Argentine

THIS PAGE Three personal images of HMS *Antelope* in San Carlos Water, taken by Marine Cole. They show the ship in normal configuration, but also the vessel's catastrophic destruction from a UXB explosion. In the panoramic black-and-white image, we can see the ship's bows slipping down beneath the water, on the right.
(Andy Cole)

air attacks is the limitations of the naval SAM systems to engage fast-moving targets coming in low over complicated terrain. The Seacat/ Sea Wolf pairing did result in kills against the attackers, although many initial kill totals were subsequently revised downward in more studied post-conflict analysis. Alastair Finlan, in his article 'War Culture: The Royal Navy and the Falklands Conflict' explains some of the issues surrounding the Seacat system:

> . . . most of the escorts in the waters around San Carlos possessed the Seacat missile system that was claimed to have achieved eight hits during the Falklands Conflict. British official sources judge this system as having had 'some success' in the campaign, but omit the critical statistic of how many missiles were fired per downed aircraft. Other sources reveal just that one out of ten Seacat missiles hit their target and that, by any standards, is a poor record. The incorporation of the Seacat missile also reduced the ability of ships to engage more than just two targets at any time, whereas the proliferation of AA guns would have allowed each individual vessel significantly better defensive firepower. Finally, had the primary defensive missile systems been knocked out, ships like the Type 21 frigate had just a 4.5-inch gun and two 20mm guns to put up a defence, apart from the volunteers on deck with small arms.

Finlan's analysis is borne out by other research, illustrating how the Seacat was in many

ABOVE HMS *Plymouth* **goes to the aid of HMS** *Antelope* **in San Carlos Water, after the latter had been hit during an Argentine air strike.** *(Defence Picture Library)*

LEFT Argentine bombs make an impact in San Carlos Water. *(Defence Picture Library)*

ways a system best suited to open-water engagements, rather than as a tool for air defence surrounding littoral operations. Sea Wolf had a somewhat better performance, killing at least four Argentine aircraft (*Brilliant* accounted for two A-4B Skyhawks of the Fuerza Aérea Argentina Grupo 5 off Stanley on 12 May, and one other aircraft flew into the sea while trying to evade a missile). Yet even then, given the scale of the British losses, it is clear that there were some critical gaps in air defence, gaps that the Argentine pilots understood and exploited to the full, with tragic consequences.

Naval gunfire support

NGS provided a powerful, if at times sporadic, artillery contribution to British ground forces operations on the Falklands. The double-gun Mk 6 and single-barrel auto-loading Mk 8 4.5in guns aboard the Royal Navy frigates and destroyers offered some advantages over the land-based artillery systems. The range of the guns was greater; a Mk 8 round, for example, could be fired over 17 miles (27km), while a 105mm Light Gun round had a maximum range of about 10.5 miles (17km). This range potential, plus the fact that the NGS platforms could be manoeuvred to firing positions around the Falklands coastline, meant that naval fire could reach any part of the island. The naval guns also delivered a greater rate of

fire per barrel; while a well-oiled gun crew could send out 6–8 rounds per minute from a 105mm gun, the Mk 8 was capable of firing 25 rounds per minute, enabling it to put more weight of shell on target in a given time.

The main issue with NGS on the Falklands was simply the availability of ships to take their place on the gunline. Only a certain number of ships carried the 4.5in guns and were configured to deliver NGS (none of the Type 22 or Leander-class frigates had guns heavier than 40mm cannon), and for those vessels NGS was purely an ancillary role that played second fiddle to the many other demands on their time. For example, it was more important for destroyers and frigates armed with modern SAM systems to maintain their role as part of the air-defence screen for the carriers and other vessels, hence the Type 42 destroyers were rarely applied to NGS. Thus the bulk of the NGS work fell upon the County-class destroyers and the Type 21 and modified Type 12 destroyers, with *Arrow*, *Avenger*, *Glamorgan* and *Yarmouth* being the most heavily used in this capacity.[7]

When organising the NGS gunline, the ships were typically in a paired arrangement, with one ship armed with the Mk 6 and the other with the Mk 8. This arrangement was partly to compensate for each gun's limitations. The double-barrelled Mk 6, for example, was capable of a greater overall rate of fire per minute, while the Mk 8 fired faster per barrel, and also had better range (by about

4,000yd/3,658m) and accuracy. Yet the Mk 8 had some reliability issues, mainly centred upon the recoil mechanism, so if a Mk 8 gun suddenly went down, the Mk 6 was there to ensure unbroken firepower delivered onshore.

The fire control for the NGS was provided by five NGSFO teams, provided by 148 Commando Forward Observation Battery. They communicated with other members of 148 Battery aboard the warships, these individuals acting as naval liaison. Overall control of the NGS was split between Rear Admiral Woodward, who assigned the number of ships to the gunline, and, initially, Brigadier Julian Thompson of 3 Cdo Bde, aided by the commanding officer of 29 Cdo Regt, RA; the land forces officers defined the fire missions. Later the control of fire passed to Major General Jeremy Moore, the Commander, Land Forces, Falkland Islands, and Colonel B.T. Pennicott, Commander Royal Artillery.

The Falklands War was a crucial experience in the history of the post-1945 Royal Navy. It was the first major conflict in which the modern Royal Navy had combat-tested its systems against another professional navy and air force. Many of the lessons that came from conflict

were sobering; the sheer level of naval losses was unexpected and startling, slapping away any last shreds of complacency and forcing a fundamental rethink about future naval development and capabilities. But the fact remained that the Royal Navy, supported by the RFA and merchant marine, had provided the means of power projection, without which the Falkland Islands could not have been retaken.

ABOVE Type 21 frigate HMS *Ardent* pictured in heavy seas during its passage through the South Atlantic. The frigate provided escort for the carriers *Hermes* and *Invincible*, and sat in San Carlos Water to provide anti-air protection for the STUFT shipping. *Ardent* was sunk on 21 May by bombs dropped from Argentine Skyhawks and Mirages. *(Defence Picture Library)*

LEFT RFA *Sir Galahad* in the process of being abandoned after being hit by an Argentine 1,000lb bomb – a UXB – on 24 May in San Carlos Water. *(Andy Cole)*

Chapter Five

Land forces – kit and equipment

In the broadest terms, there was little qualitative distinction between the land forces weapons, kit and equipment of the British Army and Royal Marines and those of the enemy they faced. The processes of NATO standardisation in the Western hemisphere, plus the commercial dominance of certain military manufacturers, meant that from the 1950s to the 1980s there had been a steady homogenisation of equipment systems among land forces. There were some weapons, vehicles and pieces of kit, however, that made all the difference in battle.

OPPOSITE **With ultra-low ground pressure, Bv 202s could go where even Land Rovers were unable (note the Land Rover sitting off to the side of the boggy track).** (Defence Picture Library)

NATO standardisation brought most of the Western world roughly into alignment in terms of land forces kit and equipment. There were exceptions – the US adoption of the 5.56mm M16 assault rifle versus the general leaning towards 7.62mm battle rifles in European and South American armed forces, for example – but the *capabilities* of the equipment were roughly similar.

Differences in naval and aviation equipment are obviously much more dramatic, and are generally far more connected to the absolute figure of defence spending rather than defence spending expressed as a percentage of GDP. Around 1982, both British and Argentine defence spending totalled about 5.5% of

GDP, but the United Kingdom was the fifth largest economy in the world, with a GDP of more than £484 billion, while Argentina was in 21st position, with a GDP of £84 billion. Nevertheless, when it came to the infantry war, the disparities between the opposing armed services were heavily ironed flat by the disparities in operational circumstances (the British having to transport all their equipment across thousands of miles of ocean, for example), plus the point of historical evolution in land forces equipment.

In this chapter we examine the critical systems that enabled British and Argentine soldiers to operate and fight in the Falklands theatre. The bulk of the chapter is focused on British kit and equipment. This weighting is not necessarily down to lack of sources, but largely because the commonality between the two armies means that it is largely easier to describe the British systems, then merely point out the differences for the Argentine forces.

Small arms

The standard British Army combat rifle of the Falklands War was the 7.62 × 51mm L1A1, a variant of the Belgian FN FAL, one of the most successful small arms of the post-war era and the first rifle issued to British troops not actually created within the UK. The original FAL was designed for simplicity, power and rugged reliability. It is a gas-operated weapon, the action operated by a short-stroke piston mechanism driving a rotating bolt. Standard feed is a 20-round box magazine, and the original Belgian FAL – and many of its international variants – had both semi-automatic and full-auto fire-selection options. Full-auto fire from a 7.62mm shoulder-mounted weapon, with a fixed-barrel, is rather an ambitious prospect, as there is excessive muzzle climb from the recoil, disrupting accuracy. In semi-auto mode, however, the FAL has a commanding capability, its iron sights (aperture rear, front post) producing tight groupings in well-trained hands out to 328yd (300m), the accuracy maintained out to 656yd (600m) and beyond. Field stripping had a simplicity to rival that of the AK-47, the FAL's main competitor for global orders.

BELOW The L1A1 Self-Loading Rifle (SLR) was an excellent battle rifle, its heavy weight and lack of full-auto fire traded against its penetration, long reach and reliability. *(Defence Picture Library)*

The FAL entered production in the early 1950s, and such was its success that it quickly expanded from a single weapon to a derivative family, the family members including folding-stock versions with short barrels (for airborne and vehicular use) and heavy-barrelled bipod-mounted versions for a moderate support-fire capability.

The British adoption of the rifle came in 1954 as the L1A1, licence-produced in the UK with the weapon's dimensions subtly modified from European metric to British imperial. While the base rifle offered little in the way of criticism, the British did make some sage modifications before it was taken into service. The most significant of these was the removal of the full-auto option, it being deemed as contributing nothing towards accuracy and practical effect on target and everything towards excessive ammunition consumption. Other tweaks were less dramatic, but showed a genuine battlefield awareness. These included:

- a folding cocking handle (the non-folding variant often snagged on clothing);
- a long flash suppressor at the muzzle;
- modifications to the receiver, bolt and bolt carrier to make it better able to cope with sand and dirt intrusion;
- deletion of the bolt hold-open device (it is debatable whether this was an advantage or disadvantage);
- larger mag release and change lever, and a folding trigger guard for using the rifle while wearing heavy gloves;
- a distinctive folding carrying handle, which sat just at the front of the receiver.

The rifle's furniture on the first generations of the L1A1 – many of which were still in service in the Falklands – was of varnished wood, but later weapons featured synthetic Maranyl furniture, a nylon 6-6 and fibreglass composite with a non-slip pebbled surface.

In many ways, the L1A1 was the perfect rifle for the Falklands War. Its durability meant that it could cope with the cold, snow, dirt and rain of the theatre, while its range meant that it could express its influence across the wide-open terrain. The penetration of the 7.62mm round also meant that it could drive through sandbags

and other defensive structures with a bit of persistent fire. It was not, however, the only rifle in British hands on the Falklands. Many SF soldiers and some RM elements opted to carry the 5.56 × 45mm M16A1, as used by the US armed forces, or the CAR-15 carbine from the same family. The M16A1 did not quite possess the reliability of the L1A1, and its field-stripping procedures were comparatively complex, but it was shorter and lighter in terms of the unloaded weapon – 6.3lb (2.86kg) as against 9.56lb (4.3kg) for the L1A1. Its ammunition was also lighter, which meant that more cartridges could be carried for the same weight. It also had a full-auto fire capability, which could be useful once the combat moved to close quarters. One

BELOW An SF unit conducts Mountain and Arctic Warfare (M&AW) training. All are armed with M16s, with extended 30-round magazines. The M16 was a far lighter option for covert operations compared to the SLR. *(Defence Picture Library)*

ABOVE A Marine displays a Starlight image-intensifying scope atop his M16 rifle. In the Falklands, such scopes were more commonly seen on SLRs or purpose-designed sniper rifles. (Defence Picture Library)

dirt or dust out via vent holes. It had nothing like the range or power of the L1A1, but at its sight-set ranges of 100–200m, and especially in the confines of position fighting, it provided a valuable local force multiplier. Some SF also used the suppressed L34A1 variant, which featured a large diffuser tube around the barrel (drilled through with 72 holes to permit gas escape). The L34A1 offered an appreciable sound reduction – even on full-auto fire the most salient noise is just that of the bolt and cocking handle oscillating – but the reduction in gas pressure at the muzzle dropped the weapon's muzzle velocity by nearly 328ft/sec (100m/sec), which meant that the weapon was really only practical in the 55–109yd (50–100m) range bracket. Once the need for stealth had passed, it appears that many SF troops resorted back to L1A1 firepower.

The standard section support weapon for the British troops was the 7.62mm L7A1 General-Purpose Machine Gun, the 'GPMG' abbreviation producing the affectionate 'Jimpy' nickname. The GPMG was also from the FN stable, being the British variant of the FN MAG. It is a gas-operated belt-fed weapon, the working parts being a successful fusion of proven designs, including those from the German MG42 and the American Browning Automatic Rifle (BAR). The standard British infantry weapon fed from metal-link belts at a rate of 850 rounds per minute, firing either from the integral bipod (its standard section mount) or, for sustained-fire operations, from a tripod. The L7A1 made a telling contribution to the firepower of the British section during the Falklands War, delivering heavy suppression and destruction at ranges well in excess of 1,093yd (1,000m). Its integral gas regulator, which allowed the operator to increase the gas flow as the weapon became dirty, a quick-change barrel, plus its generally robust construction, produced a true workhorse machine gun for the British armed services.

It was not alone in the support-fire role. Section firepower was also often boosted by the venerable Bren machine gun, albeit in the updated 7.62mm L4 variant (as opposed to its original .303in calibre). The Bren was an excellent gun, utterly proven in the Second World War and beyond, and it continued to give good service in 7.62mm format. Although it had,

reported problem, however, was that 'Round 5.56mm Ball, M193' (used by the British from 1980) did not carry the penetration or in some cases the anti-personnel effect of the heavier 7.62mm round, a debate that still dogs 5.56mm weapons to this day.

The Falklands War was also one of the last conflicts in which submachine guns (SMGs) appeared in the hands of British troops as standard issue. The L2A3 Sterling was largely issued as a firearm to support services personnel – engineers, signallers, MILAN (Missile d'infanterie léger antichar; English: light anti-tank infantry missile) operators, artillerymen, etc. – and some officers, but it did make frequent appearances as part of regular section firepower. It was a 9 × 19mm Parabellum gun with a folding stock and fired from a 34-round detachable box magazine at a cyclical rate of 550 rounds per minute. Like the L1A1, it was a robust firearm – special clearance ribs machined into the receiver worked to expel any

like the L7, a quick-change barrel, the fact that it fired largely from its own bipod (although it was also pintle-mounted on vehicles and ships) and was magazine fed – either from 30-round boxes or from standard L1A1 magazines – meant that it was a light machine gun (LMG) in tactical categorisation, ideal for proving instant support fire at the front of the advance, rather than a GPMG whose fire roles could switch considerably depending on mount options. At the other end of the scale was the .50-cal Browning M2HB. Tripod- or vehicle-mounted, the HMG had a range in excess of 2,187yd (2,000m), and was primarily used for long-range direct or indirect fire against reinforced ground positions, vehicles or as an AA weapon. The .50-cal round offered exceptional penetration against typical material defences (sandbags, wood barricades, earth berms, light armour). On its downside, however, was the fact that it was an exceptionally heavy system – 127.87lb (58kg) with tripod – hence with the emphasis on

foot logistics during the land campaign it was unsuited to forward deployment. Most of the Brownings, therefore, were positioned around fixed defendable positions, such as amphibious landing sites and captured outposts.

The L1A1, Sterling, L7 and L4 were the mainstays of the British infantry arsenal during the Falklands conflict. Of course, there were also a variety of specialist small arms in service. Snipers were equipped with the bolt-action L42A1 rifle, a 7.62mm conversion of the Lee-Enfield No. 4 sniper rifles. Firing through its 3.5-power 'Telescope, Straight Sighting, L1A1', which included a bullet-drop compensator, the L42A1 shooter could engage targets out to 765yd (700m) and beyond, depending on the talent of the shooter and a host of other variables. The Falklands did expose the age of this weapon system, however. Its sighting system was particularly prone to fogging in wet or humid weather; that is, the climate of the Falklands.

For hand-held explosive firepower, the SAS

ABOVE The 7.62mm GPMG was the primary battlefield light infantry support weapon for British ground troops. *(Defence Picture Library)*

ABOVE A soldier of the Welsh Guards mans a tripod-mounted GPMG at San Carlos. A Sterling SMG is propped up on the kit behind. (*Defence Picture Library*)

MORTARS

The British battlegroups on the Falklands typically had organic/self-observed fire support from mortar companies, which utilised the L9A1 51mm mortar and the L16A1 81mm mortar. The 51mm mortar was intended for light fire support out to a maximum range of 820yd (750m), firing HE, smoke and illuminating rounds. Although the blast effect of the small 2.03lb (920g) bomb was limited, the 51mm mortar had the great advantage of being able to be carried, deployed and fired by one man (supported by ammunition carriers obviously), and it could deliver its fire at a rate of eight rounds per minute. The 81mm mortar, by contrast, had a three-man crew but a far greater capability – it could fire a 9.9lb (4.5kg) bomb out to a range of more than 5,468yd (5,000m). Accuracy in good conditions was impressive, but on the Falklands it was limited by the fact that the mortar baseplates kept sinking down into the soft, boggy earth under each instance of recoil, changing the barrel alignment each time and consequently requiring regular re-aiming, and thereby reducing the rates of fire. (In some of the later battles of the war, there were instances of British soldiers standing on the baseplates to keep the mortars steady, but some broke their ankles as the extreme vibrations of firing ran up through their feet and legs.) In many ways, however, it was mortars, machine guns and MILANs that enabled the British troops to achieve fire supremacy in the localised battles on East Falkland.

were using some of the relatively new 40mm M203 underbarrel grenade launchers, fitted to their M16A1 rifles. These weapons, which had a 164yd (150m) range and a 16ft (5m) fragmentation kill radius (causing injuries out beyond 109yd/100m), showed their capability in some SF actions, particularly during the Pebble Island raid, where they were used to disable Argentine aircraft. The M79 'Blooper' grenade launcher – essentially a single-shot 40mm break-open shotgun design – was also used as a specialist acquisition (2 Para, for example, obtained more than 20 of the weapons from the United States). The utility of the M79 was as a tool for breaking up reinforced Argentine field positions, and its maximum range was a useful 383yd (350m) – more than double that of the M203.

Close-range explosive force was provided by the copious distribution of the L2A2 fragmentation grenade, a British adoption

ABOVE British soldiers carry 81mm mortar components and ammunition to a waiting Wessex helicopter on the Falklands. *(Defence Picture Library)*

(1972) of the American M26 grenade, with some slight changes in the burn time of the friction fuse, from 4 to 5 seconds with the M26A1 to 3.6 to 5.5 seconds. The utility of the grenade on the Falklands was the time-honoured one of bunker and trench clearance, especially useful in the mountain battles around Stanley, and to provide a form of hand-thrown preparatory barrage prior to an infantry rush. Veterans of the campaign note also that when the fragmentation grenades had run out, they might resort to using the No. 80 WP (White Phosphorus) grenades, which caused casualties primarily through burns and smoke inhalation rather than lethal fragments.

RIGHT A Para on Mount Longdon sets up a chilly GPMG post; note how he has spare ammo belts ready in cloth bandoliers. *(Defence Picture Library)*

Force multipliers – missile systems

When we refer to land forces missile systems, we are really acknowledging two categories – anti-tank missiles and surface-to-air missiles (SAMs). Regarding the former, Argentine armour was one element largely absent from the Falklands battlefield (with some exceptions noted below), so the anti-tank missiles were heavily used in their secondary role, that of the 'bunker buster'. Three systems dominated – the Rocket 66mm HEAT L1A1, the L14A1 Carl Gustaf recoilless rifle, and the MILAN ATGM (Anti-Tank Guided Missile). The Rocket 66mm HEAT L1A1 was essentially the American M72 LAW, a light single-shot disposable rocket launcher, pre-loaded with a High-Explosive Anti-Tank (HEAT) shaped-charge rocket missile. The real value of the LAW was its convenience – it weighed just 5.5lb (2.5kg) and in its unarmed state had an overall length of just 24.8in (630mm). It had an effective firing range of 660ft (200m) and could penetrate 8in (20cm) of steel plate, 24in (60cm) of reinforced concrete or 5ft 9in (1.8m) of soil. These penetration figures meant that the LAW was principally applied by British ground troops to attack Argentine fixed positions from a decent stand-off range. On the downside, however, the LAW is a direct-fire weapon well within small-arms range, hence the operator had to expose himself for several perilous seconds while he attempted to take considered aim using the iron sights. It was noted in several post-action reports from 2 Para and 3 Para that using the LAW compelled the soldier to expose himself above cover to form a good sight picture, an action that resulted in a number of casualties.

The L14A1 Carl Gustaf was most memorably used during the Falklands conflict during the initial Royal Marine defence of South Georgia on 2 April, when Marine Dave Coombes used a Carl Gustaf to cripple the corvette *Guerrico*,

holing the ship below the waterline and putting its main gun out of action. An 84mm weapon working on recoilless rifle principles, the Carl Gustaf was a Swedish anti-tank system produced by Bofors and adopted by the British Army as a section anti-tank weapon. It had a better range than the LAW – up to 765yd (700m) for fixed targets, although 300–500m was more practical – it could still be fired from the shoulder from a variety of postures, plus there was also the option of firing from a supplied bipod mount for greater accuracy. In addition it was a multi-shot weapon, and with a two-man team (gunner and loader) it could achieve a rate of fire of 6 rounds per minute. And yet, the Carl Gustaf actually had, according to many sources, little overall application in the campaign. It was heavier than the LAW at 19lb (8.5kg), which might sound manageable, but that was in addition to the many other pounds of burden the British soldier laboured under, plus this did not include the ammunition. Veteran memories of the weapon on modern social media sites often speak with contempt about the weapon, on account of its weight but also because of its exceptionally forceful report, which left ringing ears and, according to some, even nosebleeds. Indeed, in the march down from San Carlos to Stanley, many units abandoned the Carl Gustaf in preference for taking additional quantities of ammunition for the L7 machine guns and the MILAN.

A French design adopted by the British in the 1970s, the MILAN fired a 103mm-calibre missile, but unlike the LAW and the M79, the missile was guided to target by a wire-guided semi-automatic command to line-of-sight (SACLOS) system, the operator using a joystick on the launch unit to fly the missile on to target with impressive point accuracy. It also had a range of up to 1.2 miles (2km), meaning that the operator could largely stay out of range of small-arms fire if it was operationally possible. Add in the thermal-imaging sight options, for night fighting, and its impressive penetration (13.8in/352mm of rolled homogeneous armour) and the MILAN was a superb bunker-buster on the Falklands. This being said, the missile launcher and missiles combined were a logistical burden on the troops who had to carry them miles across the rough terrain.

The air-defence controversy

In terms of British anti-aircraft defence, beyond the copious volumes of small-arms fire, the main systems in operation were the Rapier and the Blowpipe. The Rapier, adopted in 1972, was a missile system intended for medium-range strategic interceptions, with an operational ceiling of 9,842ft (3,000m); 30mm cannon were meant to provide low-altitude fire, while the English Electric Thunderbird was intended for high-altitude targets. The Rapier unit consisted of a wheeled four-missile launcher, the launcher unit including a search radar dish, an 'Identification Friend or Foe' (IFF) system, the guidance computer and parabolic antenna for sending guidance commands to the missile. Guidance was by SACLOS, the

controller keeping the target tracked visually to fly the missile on to it via wireless commands.

The Shorts Blowpipe was a shoulder-launcher SAM used by the Army and Royal Marines from 1975, designed for ranges of 0.3–2 miles (0.5–3.5km). It was a single-shot unit, the launcher coming pre-loaded with the missile and fitted with necessary guidance and control electronics. The guidance system was largely similar to that of the Rapier, in that the operator had to keep visual acquisition of the target aircraft and would use a small, thumb-operated joystick to fly the missile to the contact point.

Analysis of both the Rapier and Blowpipe in the Falklands War has not been kind to their technological and tactical reputations (with absolutely no discredit to their crews, however). Soaked in seawater spray during their journey to the Falklands, the Rapiers were found to suffer from a range of reliability issues, particularly in terms of their electronics and the availability of spare parts, plus some embarrassing issues such as degraded missile retaining pins suddenly breaking and dropping the missiles on to the ground. On the first day of deployment ashore, eight of the launchers were discovered to be out of service at any time. Furthermore, the immediate post-war kill figures of 14 kills and 6 probables were subsequently revised dramatically downward to single figures, as the Falklands official history has explained, in a statement that also questions the success rates of the Blowpipe:

Within the total only five Argentine aircraft might have been shot down by Rapier, and, as originally noted by Ethell and Price, only one of these was certain, with two probables and two possibles. Similar discrepancies arose over other weapons systems, notably Blowpipe (one confirmed kill as against nine confirmed and two probables in the White Paper) and Seacat (zero to one against eight confirmed and two probables in the White Paper). [. . .] This confirmation that the MoD had exaggerated, however unwittingly, the capabilities of Rapier was deemed to be political dynamite. It was observed that if this assessment became publicly known it 'could have a serious adverse effect on sales' prospects for Rapier, which is the staple revenue-earner for BAe's Dynamic Group.[1]

So what was happening to cause the disparity between such high expectations for the missile systems and such poor results? One of the critical factors for both Rapier and Blowpipe missile operators was that the window for target acquisition and tracking was painfully short over the Falklands' complicated coastline, as Argentine aircraft typically made fast, low-level approaches, culminating in bomb-run exposures of just seconds as they flew across relatively small bays. This famously led to Julian Thompson saying that attempting to engage the jets with a Blowpipe was akin to 'trying to shoot pheasants with a drainpipe'. There were also some technical and design issues. The Rapier, for example, had a relatively small warhead that relied upon striking the aircraft directly to deliver its destructive effect; the absence of a proximity fuse meant that opportunities to down aircraft were lost when missiles passed close to them, but did not achieve a hit. The problems with the air-defence missiles led to much soul-searching and redevelopment among the Western defence establishment in the months and years after the war.

One further air-defence system that saw use in the Falklands, albeit only among the SAS, was the US FIM-92 Stinger. This relatively light, shoulder-fired missile worked via the Passive Optical Seeker Technique (POST), or infrared homing, meaning that once the missile was fired it would track itself to the target, without the operator's visual content and manual guidance, to a range of about 3 miles (5km). The Stinger was a practical system, albeit one largely unproven at the time of the Falklands. It also achieved the highest kill rate per missiles deployed: of the six missiles taken into theatre, two kills were achieved, a Pucará and an Aérospatiale SA-330 Puma.

Artillery

Artillery support on the Falklands was a much-lauded aspect of the operation, seen to have a critical effect on the outcome of many battles. The main artillery elements were provided by the batteries of 29 Cdo Regt, RA, 29 Field Battery, 4th Field Regt, RA, plus 97 Field Battery, 4 Field Regt, RA within the 5th Inf Bde. Each battery typically included two Land Rovers and up to three 1-ton Land

BELOW A Royal Artillery Rapier air-defence unit pictured at San Carlos, setting up the target-acquisition system.
(Defence Picture Library)

Rover Light Trucks, the vehicles providing transport and recon, plus six L118 105mm Light Guns. The nature of the terrain on the Falklands, however, meant that most of the transport elements of the batteries had to be left behind, the guns instead airlifted into place beneath Sea King and Wessex helicopters and the single Chinook remaining after the sinking of the *Atlantic Conveyor*. Nevertheless, the L118 was ideal for the theatre. Weighing just 4,096lb (1,858kg), it could be brought into action from a standing start in less than a minute, and could fire to a range of more than 10.5 miles (17km) at a rate of 6–8 rounds per minute. They made a particularly impressive contribution providing support fire for the British advance on Stanley; at the most intensive phases of the action, individual guns were firing more than 400 rounds per day, and in total some 30 guns put 17,500 rounds on to Argentine positions around the capital. This was in addition to the heavy offshore bombardment provided by the Royal Navy. The field artillery

fire was also highly accurate, thanks to the efficient and professional working relationship between gun crews and Forward Observation Officers (FOOs). So great was the confidence and competence of the FOOs, that in some engagements, such as those on Mount Harriet and Mount Longdon, the FOOs brought in 'danger close' fires to within 100yd (91m) of the British troops. Nick Vaux, Commanding Officer of 42 Commando, remembered both the accuracy and also the effect on target of the British artillery:

On the Gunner net the urgent, precise voice of Chris Romberg could be heard constantly designating new targets for our guns. Their fire was being brought down with unerring accuracy almost onto the assaulting groups of marines. Afterwards, none of us doubted the decisive role our gunners had played in this battle. Over 1,000 shells or bombs would fall on 'Zoya' alone that night, all of them instantly, precisely laid to cover

BELOW A non-Falklands photograph of the 105mm L118 in action. The main shell fired on the Falklands was the L31 HE round, filled with 5.5lb (2.5kg) RDX/TNT mix. *(Defence Picture Library)*

movement, suppress defensive fire, break up resistance. They gave us an overwhelming advantage, only too evident from the shattered enemy strong points, the twitching, cowed prisoners so terrified of their own incoming artillery.[2]

Artillery was considered one of the true tactical success stories of the Falklands War, and an object lesson in how to provide influential fire support to infantry under fluid assault conditions.

Armour

Although the British Army's Cold War outlook and NATO responsibilities in Europe meant that it was a heavily armoured force, the premium on shipping space and weight, plus the theatre conditions, meant that no MBTs were shipped to the theatre. Instead, four Scorpions, four Scimitars and one Samson armoured recovery vehicle (ARV) were deployed, the tracked and gunned vehicles by

ABOVE A view of the muzzle end of the 105mm L118 Light Gun, the principal artillery piece for land forces during the Falklands campaign. *(Defence Picture Library)*

BELOW L118 guns lay down a barrage during a training exercise, the photo illustrating the small ground footprint of the guns when set up. *(Defence Picture Library)*

RIGHT Although
a post-Falklands
photograph, this
Scimitar is actually a
veteran of the 1980s
conflict. Note the
clustered smoke-
grenade launchers
either side of the
RARDEN cannon.
(Defence Picture Library)

the Blues & Royals (Royal Horse Guards and
1st Dragoons) (RHG/D) cavalry regiment and
the ARV by the Royal Electrical and Mechanical
Engineers (REME). All three vehicles belonged to
the Combat Vehicle Reconnaissance (Tracked)
– CVR(T) – family, which was developed from
the 1950s for light reconnaissance and air
deployability (weight was kept to a minimum
by using aluminium armour). The Scorpion and
Scimitar had largely the same family hull and
turret configuration, the defining difference being
that the Scorpion was armed with a 76mm
cannon, firing HE, High-Explosive Squash Head
(HESH), smoke and anti-personnel canister
rounds, while the Scimitar had the fast-firing
30mm RARDEN cannon, with single-shot or
three-round-burst fire options.

The Falklands theatre offered the Blues &
Royals the opportunity to demonstrate what
light armour could contribute to the infantry
battle, but at first there was confusion over its
operational capabilities. Some commanders
believed that the soft, boggy ground would
lead to sunken and stuck vehicles. Thus the

Scorpions and Scimitars were largely used at
first to move heavy supplies around the landing
zone. The apprehensions about mobility were,
however, completely unfounded, as the broad
tracks and low vehicle weight meant that the
vehicles actually exerted less ground pressure
per inch than an adult human foot. (This was
literally demonstrated when one Blues & Royals
commander jumped down from his vehicle and
sank up to his knees in the peaty earth, while
the vehicle remained safely on the surface.)
Once it was realised that the CVR(T)s could
operate inland, they were eventually used
in their intended aggressive reconnaissance
role, fighting in support of the Scots Guards
at Mount Tumbledown and 2 Para at Wireless
Ridge. The vehicles were able to put down
heavy and highly accurate suppressive fire,
blasting emplacements apart with their main
armament before engaging flushed-out
Argentine personnel with co-axial machine
guns. The vehicles also brought the advantage
of night-vision optics, meaning that they were
fully operational during the hours of darkness.

Mention should also be made of the highly useful Bv 202, a tracked Swedish all-terrain vehicle used extensively by the Royal Marines, particularly in Arctic theatres. It was purely a logistical vehicle, used for transporting supplies and men, but its exceptionally low ground pressure meant that it could go almost anywhere on the Falklands, and certainly across ground inaccessible even to Land Rovers.

Communications

For inter-service and global communications, the UK, like all other nations with advanced armies, relied upon satellite comms, but the Falkland Islands were out of range of the Skynet 2B satellite that enabled comms in much of the rest of the world. Instead, a cornerstone of long-range communications was the Royal Navy's Satellite Communications Onboard Terminal (SCOT), which could connect with other networks, such as the US Defense Satellite Communications System (DSCS). For the land forces, strategic comms were supported by Racal SC 2600 satellite net station established at Ajax Bay.

ABOVE A CVR(T) armoured recovery vehicle (ARV) in Stanley, just after the end of hostilities. *(Defence Picture Library)*

Yet the most crucial volume of communications, both within land forces units and between land, air and sea assets, was conducted at the tactical level on radios on HF, VHF and UHF bands. For the British Army

LEFT Army/Marine Scout helicopters provided CASEVAC, resupply and SF insertion/extraction support to British land forces on the Falklands. *(Defence Picture Library)*

Band	Model	Range	Notes
HF	UK/PRC 320	25 miles (40km) (daylight); 31–1,243 miles (50–2,000km) at night using 'Skywave'	Man-portable; issued at company level
HF	UK/VRC 321	25 miles (40km) (daylight); 31–1,243 miles (50–2,000km) at night using 'Skywave'	Vehicle-mounted; for inter-company comms outside range of VHF net
HF	UK/VRC 322	25+ miles (40km+) (daylight); 31–1,243 miles (50–2,000km) at night using 'Skywave'	Vehicle-mounted; teletype plus voice transmissions
VHF	PRC 349	0.6 miles (1km)	Man-portable; personal comms within infantry section
VHF	PRC 350	1+ mile (1.6km+)	Man-portable; intra-platoon backpack; extended range version of PRC 349
VHF	PRC 351/352	5 miles (8km) (PRC 351); 10 miles (16km) (PRC 352)	Man-portable; intra-platoon backpack; PRC 352 features additional power unit to boost signal strength and range
VHF	PRC 353	20 miles (32km)	Vehicle-mounted; voice, teletype and digital transmissions
UHF	UK/PRC 344	100 miles (160km)	Ground-to-air communications

BELOW WO1 Pat Chapman leads Marines of 42 Cdo out of San Carlos across the Falklands. Note the M16 rifle he carries, only used by some Marines and by SF. *(Defence Picture Library)*

and Commandos, comms were supplied via the Clansman Combat Net Radio (CNR), a family of nine individual radio sets that had been introduced in 1976 as a replacement for the Larkspur system (although some Larkspur sets were in evidence during the Falklands campaign). The Clansman CNR offered a broad spectrum of communication ranges and capabilities, from intra-section voice comms of less than a mile through to theatre digital, teletype and digital transmission over ranges of more than 100 miles (160km); the range of radios could be increased, sometimes massively, by reflecting or refracting radio waves off the ionosphere, particularly at night, in the 'Skywave' technique.

The main problem for radio operators in the Falklands was environmental interference with the signals, especially when the weather was very wet, snowy or windy. The harsh climate was also physically hard on the radio sets, causing many malfunctions, and in severe cold battery life was significantly reduced.

Uniform and personal equipment

The foundation of uniform for British land forces during the Falklands campaign was the 1968-pattern Disruptive Pattern Material (DPM) uniform, the basic elements of which were the Smock, Combat and Trousers, Combat, both rendered in the distinctive woodland-type DPM fabric. For the smock there was also a button-on Hood, Combat, DPM, lined with green cotton. The extensive issue of DPM material by the time of the Falklands did not prevent older stocks of plain olive-green uniform being in evidence in some branches of service.

For different theatre requirements, the DPM family expanded to provide specialist clothing for certain units, much of which spread out

into the wider Army. The Smock, Windproof, Arctic and Trousers, Windproof, Arctic were issued to the Royal Marines during the 1970s, and were much in evidence throughout land forces as the weather closed in across the Falklands. Snipers and Paras also acquired specialist versions of the smock, to suit their particular operational requirements. For extra warmth, quilted overtrousers were available, which featured zipped bottoms to enable them to be pulled on over boots. A variety of fur-lined caps, mittens, gloves, scarves, balaclavas and socks completed the protection against the cold. An additional versatile piece of kit was a waterproof polyurethane-coated nylon poncho, which could swap between the roles of rain cape and bivouac shelter, depending on how it was configured.

In terms of ballistic head protection, most photographs show that Paras wore 'soft' caps or the formation berets when not in combat, but the Mk II (steel) M76 (glass-reinforced plastic) para helmets in action. The Mk II helmet, with a different liner, became the Marine Pattern Helmet. We also see some other British infantry troops in the Mk IV 'turtle' helmet, its distinctive contours somewhat obscured by DPM cover attached to most items.

One of the most controversial items of British military kit on the Falklands was the Directly Moulded Sole (DMS) boot, introduced into British service in the 1960s. Its name derived from the fact that the plastic, not leather, sole was fused directly to the upper for a highly durable fit. However, the plastic sole had extremely poor drying qualities; with a leather sole, water inside the boot could evaporate out through the porous leather, but with the DMS such water largely stayed inside, trapped by the impermeable plastic. Moreover, the tongue of the boot was low and did not prevent water from flooding in through the lace eyelets. This was a disastrous state of affairs in the Falklands, where soldiers often sank into soaking peaty ground up to their ankles with

every step. The result was that the Falklands War saw the re-emergence of trench foot, a potentially dangerous immersion skin condition that had been little seen since the days of First World War trench warfare. Once wet, the soldiers' feet were also prone to frostbite when the temperatures dipped below freezing.

It is well known that the soldiers who campaigned on the Falklands were beasts of burden, the total weight of kit and equipment carried often adding up to 80lb (36kg) and more. The principal system for carrying the load was the British Army General Service (GS) 1972-pattern rucksack plus the 1958-pattern webbing. The GS rucksack – often known as the 'Bergen'– had a body of waterproof canvas fitted to an A-frame, with padded fabric straps for fitting over the shoulders. Top and front pouches provided extra storage. Total storage was about 60 litres, but there was another version for SAS/Para troops with around double the capacity and additional pouches.

Belt kit and ammo pouches were provided by the 1958-pattern webbing. In design the 1958-pattern system was practical and useful, with ample storage, a comfortable fit and the ability to suspend additional items from the belt and straps. On the downside, the heavy cotton straps – which had the advantage of a solid grip within the strap buckles, making them less prone to slippage – absorbed and retained water, making it uncomfortable to wear for prolonged periods.

The Falklands War was a very exposed conflict for ground forces, the men frequently having to sleep out in the open under especially hostile conditions. The aforementioned poncho was often critical for providing overhead shelter (male and female stud fittings meant that several ponchos could be fitted together, or it could be pegged like a tent) or served as a groundsheet, while a sleeping roll – usually seen fitted into loops at the top of the rucksack – provided some protection against ground cold.

RIGHT AND BELOW Gurkha soldiers show a variety of kit and clothing items, including the standard DPM uniform, the British Army waterproof poncho, and the fur-lined Cap, Combat, Arctic, DPM. *(Defence Picture Library)*

For sleeping, there were a variety of sleeping bags available, but the most common was the Combat and General Service (GS) bag, which was filled with a 50/50 mix of waterfowl down and feathers. One of its great features for the Falklands campaign was the integral waterproof groundsheet, plus the integral hood. Once ensconced inside, the soldier could expect to stay reasonably warm.

Argentine distinctions

While our focus so far has been largely on British land forces, some key points of distinction with the Argentines are warranted. A comparison of kit and equipment, however, indicates as many areas of overlap

and commonality as there are differences. For example, the Argentine soldiers were also evidently equipped with the same family of FN small arms. Licensed production of the FAL began in 1960 in Argentina, in folding-stock FAL 50.61 battle rifle (with full-auto fire selection retained) and heavy-barrel FAL 50.41 support variants. Other small arms in the Argentine arsenal, identical with those of the British, included the M16A1, Sterling SMG, the FN MAG and the Browning M2HB. Differences included the PAM 1 and PAM 2 (variants of the US M3 'Grease Gun'), Uzi SMGs and the 7.62mm Beretta BM-59E rifle. They operated 60mm, 81mm, 107mm and 120mm mortars for support fire, plus the US M40 90mm and M68 recoilless rifles; by the time of the Falklands War these vintage weapons were looking a little dated, but they could deliver a respectable punch over the 90mm's 1,640yd (1,500m) and the 105mm's 10,061yd (9,200m) effective ranges.

One area in which the Argentines were in complete contrast to the British was in their prolific use of landmines on the approaches to bases and positions. Both anti-personnel and anti-tank mines were sown, in a total of 117 minefields covering almost 8 square miles (20km^2). In the immediate months after the war,

British Army engineers cleared some 4,500 mines at the cost of two dead, but even today signs emblazoned with the message 'Danger! Mines!' dot the Falklands landscape.

For air defence, the Argentine forces were, like the UK, users of the Blowpipe system. They also had supplies of the Soviet 9K32 Strela-2 (NATO reporting name: SA-7 Grail) man-portable missiles, channelled to Argentina via Libya; these fired a passive infra-red homing missile at an effective range of 2.3 miles (3.7km), and therefore presented a threat to low-altitude strike aircraft, although none of the missiles appear to have been fired in the conflict. Of more significance was the single Roland missile system deployed around Stanley airfield. This French system again had a relatively short range – up to 3.4 miles (5.5km) – but that was sufficient to push British aircraft to higher operational altitudes, and thus compromise the accuracy of the bombing, in these days when most munitions dropped remained of the 'dumb' unguided type. The other SAM system used by the Argentines was the Tigercat – the land-based version of the naval Seacat – actually a British design with a range similar to that of the Roland. Unlike the Roland, which was guided by tracking radar, the

Tigercat was controlled visually through CLOS via a radio link. The system was not particularly effective, although one missile inflicted damage on a Harrier via a near miss on 12 June.

In addition to the missiles in service, for short-range air defence the Argentines also deployed significant AA cannon systems, including 15 Rheinmetall 20mm/75 anti-aircraft guns, about 20 Hispano-Suiza 832 30mm guns and 15 Oerlikon GDF-002 35mm twin cannon. The largest of these, the 35mm gun, had a maximum effective range of 4,374yd (4,000m). The cannon could be allied to radar fire-control systems, making them highly accurate, and the barrels could also be depressed to allow the guns to function in the ground-fire role.

The Argentine forces also differed significantly to the British in armour and artillery. Regarding armour, it is interesting how minor a role Argentine armoured vehicles played in the conflict, at least after the opening invasion, in which amphibious LTVP-7 and LARC-5 vehicles were used to deploy troops to shore. Twelve Panhard AML-90 90mm 4 × 4 Armoured Cars were deployed around Stanley, although it was quickly ascertained that they were only capable of moving along metalled roads, thus many of their crews ended up being redeployed as infantry.

For artillery, the two principal instruments were, for field artillery support, the Oto Melara M56 105mm Pack Howitzer, and, for heavy artillery support, the CITER 155mm L33 Gun. Interestingly enough, the highly portable M56 Pack Howitzer had also been in British service until it was replaced by the L118 Light Gun. Its light weight of 2,840lb (1,290kg), excellent transportability, rapid rate of fire (10 rounds per minute) and 6-mile (10km) effective range made it a respected piece of kit, but one that struggled to maintain reliability in hard field conditions. The L33 was an indigenous artillery piece, at least four of which were deployed to the Falklands. As they had a 12-mile (20km) range, the main intention behind their use was to provide counterfire against British offshore naval bombardment, but they were also heavily used against the British advances on Stanley.

What is apparent from this overview of British and Argentine infantry weapons and kit is that neither side had a clear superiority in any regard, at least from a technological point of view. Above all else, it would therefore be tactics that would decide the battles.

BELOW The Argentine Panhard AML-90 4 × 4 vehicle had the potential to be a problem for British forces on the Falklands, but ultimately the armoured vehicles were scarcely used owing to mobility and tactical issues. *(Rama/ CC-BY-SA-2.0-FR)*

Chapter Six

Amphibious assault and setting up bases

On 21 May 1982, the Task Force's Amphibious Group began the first definitive step in the recapture of the Falkland Islands, with the major amphibious landing operation of Royal Marines and Paras at San Carlos Water. The outcome of this operation, given the limited planning time, sketchy intelligence and scant rehearsals, was unpredictable, and the near-certain possibility of a heavy Argentine air response genuinely threatened its success. Yet the landings went ahead as planned, and established the key foothold on the islands, despite the subsequent efforts of the Argentine jets to break the British grip.

OPPOSITE **A tractor of the Commando Logistics Regiment ferries stores off an LCU.** *(Defence Picture Library)*

117

Operation Paraquet

The San Carlos landings were not the first British amphibious action of the war, however. Properly codenamed Operation Paraquet (a variant spelling of 'Parakeet') – but more popularly labelled Operation Paraquat, after a brand of rat poison, the action to retake South Georgia between 21 and 26 April was in fact an earlier land victory for the British. It was undoubtedly a close-run thing, however, as much characterised by muddled planning and some chronic misjudgements as it was by bravery and adaptive thinking.

The force assembled for the taking of South Georgia was CTG 317.9, which initially consisted of the County-class destroyer *Antrim*, the Type 12 frigate *Plymouth* and the oiler *Tidespring*, with overall command of the Task Force falling to Captain Brian Young aboard *Antrim*. The principal land forces element within the formation was M Company, 42 Cdo (aboard *Tidespring*), with 2 SBS attached. Command of this group was under Major Guy Sheridan, 2-in-C

of 42 Cdo and an expert in mountain warfare. The task group was later joined by D Sqn SAS led by Major Cedric Delves, who joined CTG 317.9 from Ascension Island via the *Fort Austin*. On 14 April the task group linked up with *Endurance*, Captain Barker and his crew bringing their expert understanding of South Georgia to the planning process.

The strategy for the retaking of South Georgia seems to have been fraught with inter-service rivalry, particularly between the SAS on one side and the Marines/SBS on the other, with various experts caught in the crossfire. An operation eventually emerged, albeit one in which the Marine contingent from M Coy – previously earmarked as the main force for Paraquet – was effectively sidelined as a reserve in favour of SF (or 'Advanced Forces', as they were known) taking the lead. The plan was essentially divided into two phases: 1) North of Grytviken, the 12-man SAS Mountain Troop would be landed by helicopter on the Fortuna Glacier, roughly 10 miles (16km) from Leith, and would advance from there to

recce Leith, Stromness and Husvik, and 2) South of Grytviken, 2 SBS would be landed at Hound Bay, cross the Cumberland Bay East by Gemini boat, and recce Grytviken itself. It should be noted that some individuals with deep experience of South Georgia's climate and terrain, including Captain Barker of *Endurance* and Dr Richard Law, the BAS director, felt that the SAS part of the mission did not take adequate account of the terrain and climate involved, and thereby was excessively risky.

The deployments began in the early morning of 21 April, but were problematic from the start on account of a screaming South Atlantic blizzard that was sweeping through the region. After one aborted helicopter landing attempt, three Wessex helicopters – led by Lieutenant Commander Ian Stanley flying 'Humphrey' from *Antrim* – managed to put the SAS Mountain Troop on to Fortuna Glacier. At around 05:30hrs, a four-man 2 SBS patrol was inserted at Hound Bay by Wasp helicopter, but two further patrols could not land because of the adverse weather.

ABOVE Royal Marines in full Arctic warfare clothing raise the Union Flag on South Georgia. *(Defence Picture Library)*

BELOW SF soldiers on the flight deck of HMS *Antrim* off the coast of South Georgia during Operation Paraquet. *(Defence Picture Library)*

RIGHT A Royal Navy
Wessex helicopter lies
on its side on South
Georgia, having been
blown over during
attempts to extract
the SAS team from
Fortuna Glacier on
22 April. *(Defence
Picture Library)*

By 22 April, it became obvious that the SAS troops on Fortuna Glacier needed to be rescued. The deep snow, terrible visibility and glacier crevasses meant that they had made almost no physical advance, and death by hypothermia was a real possibility. In the early afternoon, three Wessex headed out for the pick-up, and boarded the soldiers, but then one of the Wessex – that from *Tidespring* flown by Lieutenant Mike Tidd – lost all visibility, went into a spin and crashed, toppling over on its side. Thankfully there were only minor injuries, but the rescue operation was now expanding. Stanley and the other Wessex pilot, Lieutenant Ian Georgeson, now picked up all the stranded personnel between them, but on the return journey Georgeson's Wessex was grounded by the weather, and then blown over in extreme winds. Stanley, performing multiple heroic flights, managed to return to the scene of the crash and rescued all the personnel, but a fruitless and ill-advised deployment had cost CTG 317.9 two of its helicopters.

The SBS action was also having its share of bad luck. The Gemini boats were flown in by two helicopters, but one was damaged beyond use and the other could not be used because Cumberland Bay was completely iced over. Later on the 22nd, therefore, the SBS troopers were extracted by helicopter. The

SAS Boat Troop, meanwhile, made a tortured Gemini deployment of their own to Grass Island in Stromness Bay; with many of the boats' outboard motors failing in the sea spray and rain, the troopers becoming dispersed.

The South Georgia attack was in danger of unravelling completely. Furthermore, it became increasingly apparent that the Argentines were well aware of the British presence around South Georgia. On 23 April the submarine *Santa Fe* was spotted around the task group, and even made torpedo lock-on on to *Endurance*, but did not fire; the next day, an Argentine Boeing 707 military reconnaissance aircraft flew directly over the task group, dropping to just 3,000ft (914m) to observe the ships. Because of the submarine threat in particular, *Antrim* and *Tidespring* withdrew out of the area. *Santa Fe*, meanwhile, anchored off Grytviken and put ashore reinforcements in the form of an additional 20 personnel, a mix of combat technicians and marines.

The fortunes of Operation Paraquet began to change on the afternoon of 24 April. *Antrim* and *Tidespring* were joined by the Type 22 frigate HMS *Brilliant*, sent by Rear Admiral Woodward to provide additional guard against submarine threats and to offer the ship's two Lynx helicopters to the faltering ground operation. The next day, *Santa Fe* was disabled in a depth-charge attack by 'Humphrey' and other helicopters, including one of *Brilliant*'s Lynx, negated the submarine threat; the British warships sailed back into the waters off South Georgia.

Captain Young now decided to force the issue on land with whatever troops he could scrape together. He put together a 'Composite Company Group' of 75 men – a mix of SBS, SAS, some Marines and NGS artillery FOs from NGFO2 and NGFO5 of the 148 (Meiktila) Commando Forward Observation Battery – under the command of Major Sheridan. The company was deployed on the afternoon of the 25th, with *Antrim* and *Plymouth* providing heavy offshore bombardment that completely shattered Argentine morale. The landing force put ashore at Hestesletten and then advanced up towards Grytviken, inadvertently engaging a force of seals on the way. As the British troops moved up into Grytviken, the call to surrender went out to the Argentines, the message reinforced by having *Antrim* sail menacingly into Cumberland Bay. After some wrangling with the

LEFT Marine 'Rocky' Rowe was guarding the Argentine submarine *Santa Fe*, after it had been crippled by helicopter assault off Grytviken, South Georgia. During this duty, he saw Argentine Navy Petty Officer Félix Artuso, whom Rowe believed was engaged in sabotage efforts, and shot the Argentine sailor dead. *(Defence Picture Library)*

BELOW The crippled Argentine submarine *Santa Fe*, clearly showing the impact points on its conning tower from the naval helicopter strikes. *(Defence Picture Library)*

RIGHT Marines patrol among the shoreline of South Georgia, having recaptured the island. There were occasions during the Falklands War when local wildlife – particularly seals and walruses – were engaged by both sides in low-visibility conditions. *(Defence Picture Library)*

BELOW Lieutenant Commander Alfredo Astiz signs the surrender agreement in the wardroom of HMS *Plymouth*, following the British recapture of South Georgia. *(Defence Picture Library)*

Argentines, particularly the force commanded by Astiz, the final white flags were raised and South Georgia was back in British hands.

Pebble Island and SF reconnaissance

Although the raid on South Georgia needed some serious after-action reflection to avoid future mistakes, British land forces had now clawed back occupied territory from the Argentines, giving a welcome boost to morale, especially after the loss of *Sheffield*. The SAS

had experienced probably the most troubled aspects of the raid, but three weeks later they were able to reassert themselves with another attack, as part of the build-up to the main landings on the Falklands.

This time the objective for D Sqn was Pebble Island, an outcrop off the north coast of West Falkland, used primarily as an air base for a mixed force of Pucará, Mentors and a Skyvan. The island was a threat to the Task Force not only for its aircraft, which would be able to launch ground-attack missions against the amphibious movements and a beachhead,

but also because by being 108 miles (174km) closer to Argentina than Port Stanley, it provided the Argentines with the best base for aerial resupply and reinforcement once the land campaign had begun in earnest. With the main landings scheduled for 21 May, scarcely more than a week away, D Sqn was given the job of negating Pebble Island as a threat.

The first SAS elements to land on the island were eight men of the Boat Troop, who deployed silently to the coastline by canoe on the night of 11/12 May. Carrying their craft across the island, the SAS troops used the canoes again to cross a stretch of water around the air base, the men then quietly emplacing themselves around the facility from select observation posts (OPs). There they monitored the activity at the air base for two days, and eventually, on the night of the 14th, they radioed *Hermes* with the message: 'Eleven aircraft. Believed real. Attack tonight.' The message was a signal to the remaining 45 men from D Sqn, supplemented by an NGSFO who was to act as a liaison for offshore NGS from HMS *Glamorgan*.

The SAS force was flown on to Pebble Island via Sea King HC.4 helicopters from No. 846 NAS from *Hermes*, the pilots wearing night-vision goggles for the midnight action. The landing zone, which had already been marked out by the advance SAS group, was some distance from the objective, hence the soldiers had to perform a long march with a groaning burden of equipment, including a mortar tube, baseplate and ammunition, GPMGs, plus copious demolition charges, intended for the aircraft.

In the early hours of the morning, the attack went in. The NGSFO brought in fire from *Glamorgan*, which rained down 4.5in shells at the rate of one per minute. The SAS team itself was split into two units. The first was a support group, whose job it was to attack the buildings and facilities housing the naval air personnel. While this suppression was under way, the second group – the attack group – was to advance on to the airfield itself and destroy the aircraft there with the demolition charges and grenades.

The mission went like clockwork. With the Argentine defenders hunkering down under small-arms fire and naval shelling, the attack group worked systematically through the parked and impotent aircraft, wrecking one after another

with the explosives. In just a few short minutes, 11 aircraft had been destroyed, plus a base radar installation, a fuel dump and an ammo store. As the SAS finally withdrew, some Argentine units began to offer more determined resistance, but the shooting down of one of their officers silenced the effort. The SAS troops and the NGSFO thereafter retreated unopposed back to their LZ, where they were extracted by helicopters.

The Pebble Island raid is a perfect example of the disruptive effect that Advanced Forces were to have during the Falklands War. Although not all information is in the public domain, it is clear that both SAS and SBS operatives were working on both East and West Falkland in the weeks prior to the main landings at San Carlos, and throughout the campaign in both reconnaissance and raiding roles. Indeed, their preparations for the missions had begun before deployment, as tensions grew in the South Atlantic. 'Baz' (full name withheld), then a young soldier in the SBS, remembered that once the Falklands conflict looked possible,

. . . everything we were doing changed. We were told that we were going to spend all our training time as a Special Forces unit on Dartmoor, around Hay Tor – there are

RIGHT Royal Marines
prepare to board
landing craft as the
embarked force of
3 Cdo Bde go ashore
at San Carlos. *(Defence
Picture Library)*

*another couple of tors around there – and
we were basically told to find out as many
different ways as we could of taking those
tors. You had to assume that there was an
enemy on them; the fouler the weather, the
more you had to do it. If the weather breaks,
then you have a rest. And you do it, and
do it, and do it again. . . . We would play
each scenario out, looking at each other's
movements and progressions.*

The preparation on Dartmoor was perfectly
matched to the type of terrain and weather that
would be encountered in the Falklands.
Baz and his team were eventually deployed
around Stanley, living for days in nothing more
than covered earth scrapes, surviving mainly on
whatever lean animals they could catch. Their
purpose, as he remembers, was principally
observation:

*We were to be the eyes and ears. We were
to dig in, observe who was coming in, who
was coming out, how many, what were their
strengths, what were they doing and report
back at every opportunity.*

The combined efforts of all the SF teams provided
critical intelligence to support the landings. But

as we shall see later, as the war developed into a
full-blown shooting match, the SF soldiers would
also be in the thick of the action.

The San Carlos landings

At the moment the Task Force ships first
set sail from the UK in April 1982, the
plans for an amphibious assault on the Falkland
Islands were in development. Intelligence about
the Argentine dispositions was limited and
patchy, and there was little time and physical
opportunity to rehearse options for attack.
Furthermore, the clock was ticking. Rear
Admiral Woodward and his staff determined
that any landing would basically have to take
place by 25 May at the latest, this allowing
the ground troops the best part of a month to
complete the job. This timescale was imperative
because by the end of June the full force of the
Falklands winter would descend, hitting ships,
aircraft and ground forces alike, plus the CVBG
would be in critical need of shore maintenance,
and the only ports that could provide that
maintenance were back in the UK. Time was
therefore not on the British side. The shortage
of days was especially concerning because
the Amphibious Group ships had not been
combat-loaded at the outset, and it would take
considerable time to cross-deck all supplies into
the appropriate vessels and rearrange them in
the right order.

A key consideration in the planning of the
landings was, of course, where to land in the
first place. In total, a list of 19 potential sites
were drawn up, and Southby-Tailyour was
consulted closely about all of them, drawing on
his excellent local knowledge. In the end, San
Carlos Bay, tucked in the north-west corner of
East Falkland, was selected for the following
reasons:

- It was far less well defended than positions
  around Port Stanley, and was also out of
  range of the Argentine artillery further south
  on the island.
- San Carlos Water offered good anchorage to
  all the Amphibious Group ships, including the
  largest of the vessels, such as *Canberra*.
- The enclosed nature of San Carlos made
  it difficult for Argentine aircraft to assault.

Approaching from either the west, directly through the neck of San Carlos, or from the east overland over Sussex Mountains, any Argentine aircraft making an attack run would have only seconds to identify a target, align the aircraft for a bomb run, and make the attack before escaping.

■ The steep shoreline gave both landing troops and ships some degree of protection from air and missile attack, a key consideration in light of recent Exocet tragedies.

But San Carlos was not perfect. Its narrow mouth, for example, made it particularly suitable for Argentine mining. It was also a long way from Stanley, and therefore increased both the overland logistical burden and the number of objectives the ground forces would have to fight before reaching the capital. There was an additional threat posed by the substantial Argentine force at Goose Green/Darwin; it was hoped that the element of surprise could be maintained to avoid the Argentines moving

up to the beachhead and preparing it for a contested landing. Yet compared to all the other alternatives, San Carlos remained the best option, and it was therefore selected. All unit commanders were briefed of this fact on 13 May, and the momentum began to build.

Planning and preparation

The landings at San Carlos were simple in outline, complex in execution. In basic principle, the Amphibious Group – operating under the CAP cover of the CVBG – would land some 3,000 Paras and Commandos. The main vessels for putting the troops ashore would be the Landing Craft Utility (LCU) Mk 9, shallow-draft amphibious craft each capable of carrying then disembarking 120 troops (or four large vehicles), via the bow ramps. Eight LCUs were deployed within the Landing Platform Docks (LPDs) HMS *Fearless* and HMS *Intrepid* – four per ship. The supply transports *Europic Ferry*, *Fort Austin*, *Sir Galahad*, *Sir Geraint*, *Sir Lancelot*, *Sir Percivale* and *Sir Tristram* would

BELOW SF personnel pictured on the deck of the assault ship **Intrepid**, with HMS **Hermes** sailing by in the background. *(Defence Picture Library)*

provide heavy logistical support and further troop transfers, with Mexeflote powered landing rafts giving further logistical transfer. Once men and logistics were on dry land, the beachhead would be steadily consolidated, with supply dumps, headquarters, medical facilities, air-defence systems and many other facilities established to provide a secure foothold for subsequent operations inland.

The San Carlos landings were scheduled for 21 May. In its initial configuration, the plan was broken down as follows:

BELOW A map of the landing beaches around San Carlos Bay. *(Defence Picture Library)*

Element	Unit	Objective
First wave	40 Cdo	Blue Beach, in the south-east corner of San Carlos Water
	45 Cdo	Red Beach, Ajax Bay
Second wave	2 Para	Sussex Mountains, south of San Carlos
	3 Para	Green Beach on the northern edge of San Carlos Water; secure Port San Carlos
Diversionary attacks	D Squadron SAS	Distract Task Force Mercedes at Goose Green, to prevent their moving up to the landing site
	HMS *Glamorgan*	Bombardment of Army Group Stanley around Berkeley Sound
Floating reserve	42 Cdo	Floating reserve aboard *Canberra*

The plan was briefed, but then had to be revised at the 11th hour when problematic intelligence came in indicating that an Argentine combat team was emplaced on Fanning Head, the northern promontory at the neck of San Carlos Water. Given the narrowness of that neck, there was a real concern that such a combat team could inflict serious casualties on the Amphibious Group as it passed into the bay, using 105mm recoilless rifles or anti-tank rocket launchers. (The early Royal Marine defence of South Georgia had proven how effective such a defence could be.) Captain Michael Clapp, in charge of the Amphibious Group landings, and Julian Thompson consulted closely and decided that a modification of the plan was required both to combat the Fanning Head threat directly, while also strengthening the beachhead against the possibility of an attack by an Argentine mobile reserve. The new plan, put together with much frustrated last-minute cross-decking, ran as follows:

Element	Unit	Objective
First wave	2 Para	Blue Beach 2, advancing quickly to Sussex Mountains to guard against threats from Goose Green
	40 Cdo	Red Beach 1 at Ajax Bay, securing the refrigeration plant
Second wave	45 Cdo	Sussex Mountains, south of San Carlos
	3 Para	Green Beach 1 at Sandy Bay, securing Port San Carlos
Fanning Head	3 SBS	Identify, attack and destroy the Argentine force on Fanning Head
Diversionary attacks	D Squadron SAS	Distract Task Force Mercedes at Goose Green
	HMS *Glamorgan*	Bombardment of Army Group Stanley around Berkeley Sound
Floating reserve	42 Cdo	Floating reserve aboard *Canberra*

ABOVE Logistics vehicles and personnel of the Commando Logistics Regiment run into San Carlos. Note the 'Eager Beaver' machine on the shoreline, fitted with a track-laying device. *(Defence Picture Library)*

In addition to these spearhead combat troops, the forces offshore in the supply transports, who would also be deployed, included:

■ 29 Cdo Regiment RA
■ 59 Independent Commando Squadron
■ Commando Brigade Air Squadron
■ Commando Logistics Regiment

■ Brigade HQ and Signals Squadron
■ Mountain & Arctic Warfare Cadre
■ 656 Squadron AAC
■ 16 Field Ambulance RAMC
■ 'T' Battery, 12 Air Defence Regiment RA.

It was with this plan that the British committed to the landings at San Carlos. Confirmation for the go-ahead was received on 20 May,

with the landings scheduled for 03:30hrs the next day. The Paras, Marines and other troops spent an uncomfortable and nervous night aboard the offshore vessels, which were terribly overcrowded. The situation had been made far worse by a Northwood decision to redistribute two of the three battalions aboard *Canberra* to *Fearless* and *Intrepid*, fearing the consequences of a devastating air attack on the liner, with its huge Skyhawk-friendly silhouette. The transfer, set against the background of much grumbling, was performed on 19–20 May, by using the LCUs to send 40 Cdo to *Fearless* and 3 Para to *Intrepid*. The result was a prodigious squeeze aboard the LPDs; *Fearless*, for example, was now housing 1,400 troops in addition to its crew, more than double the manual capacity.

The landings

The first action of the San Carlos landings began shortly after midnight on 21 May with the assault on the 'Fanning Head Mob' – the jaunty British nickname for the Argentines occupying those positions. Four Sea King lifts from *Antrim* deposited 35 men from 3 SBS and a NGS liaison team (led by noted Falklands veteran author Hugh McManners) about 3,000yd (2,743m) from Fanning Head; the SBS troops advanced with purpose

towards their contact. At about 1,000yd (914m) from the Argentine position, at 02:15hrs, McManners tried to bring in fire from *Antrim*, but a technical problem on the ship meant that the bombardment couldn't begin until about 03:15hrs, by which time the SBS troops had begun their attack at distance with mortars. Once the NGS started arriving, however, and as the SBS aggressively closed in on them, the Argentine troops were steadily thrown into disarray, although they resisted calls on them to surrender. In the darkness and gunfire-split confusion, many of the Argentine troops managed to slip away (about 80, most later captured), and 12 men had been killed, but the SBS took control of Fanning Head. Among the abandoned equipment discovered there were 105mm recoilless guns, an 81mm mortar and some Blowpipe missiles; this discovery proved that the decision to launch the raid had been a judicious one.

The raid against Fanning Head, plus the diversionary attack by the SAS at Darwin, provided some measure of distraction away from the main landings at San Carlos. The first British troops to reach the shores were, as planned, men from 2 Para and 40 Cdo, with Scimitars from the Blues & Royals providing a measure of armoured protection. Boots touched dry land at 04:00hrs, later than

planned because of delays and confusion in launching the landing parties, and had finished the transfer by 07:30hrs. The soldiers of 45 Cdo and 3 Para were also in the process of landing by 09:30hrs, and 42 Cdo – the floating reserve – also went ashore later in the day.

The landings at San Carlos had been totally uncontested, much to the relief of soldiers and planners. The Paras and Marines moved up to their designated positions around the bay and inland, to create a line of defence against possible counter-attack. There was some limited contact with Argentine forces. Soldiers of 3 Para, moving into San Carlos, encountered a force of about 40 Argentine troops there, whom they dispersed in a firefight. The 3 Cdo Bde Air Sqn suffered the first fatalities of the land campaign, when two Gazelles were shot down over San Carlos river, with three men killed.

Meanwhile, the 12 Amphibious Group ships

ABOVE Landing Craft Utility (LCUs) head for the beach at San Carlos, with LPD assault ship HMS *Fearless* in the background, as the attack takes place on the morning of 21 May 1982. *(Defence Picture Library)*

LEFT A Sea King helicopter brings in supplies to the Commando logistics hub established at Ajax Bay. *(Andy Cole)*

ABOVE *Intrepid*
and *Fearless* make
a swift move out of
San Carlos Water as
a red alert comes
in, warning of an
impending Argentine
air attack. *(Andy Cole)*

had moved into San Carlos Water and, as the Argentines became fully alert to the landings there, began to experience the horror of unrelenting air attacks. Over the next few days, the soldiers on shore would be both spectators and targets for enemy air activity. Andy Cole, a Marine with the Commando Logistics Regiment, remembers one incident:

RIGHT Troops from
5 Inf Bde – Welsh
Guards and Scots
Guards – are ferried
ashore by LCU.
(Defence Picture Library)

We were caught out in the open. I was with a mate and we were going out to resupply the guys who were in the trenches, dug in. These two Skyhawks came in and I thought 'They're going for us.' And I can remember hiding under my cagoule on this hillside – completely helpless. Anyway, they just roared overhead and left us alone – they were just trying to sink the ships in San Carlos and Ajax Bay.

What became apparent to the British troops, however, was that there were indeed several Argentine OPs around San Carlos, which were acting as FOs for the air strikes. Andy Cole again remembers:

They had an OP on Ajax Bay which we only became aware of because I was on the flight deck on *Sir Galahad*, and I caught a glint of light flashing off some binoculars. I reported this to my sergeant-major, and told him that there was someone watching us from over the hillside there. It took more information than that before we realised that the Argentines had a really professional OP calling in the aircraft onto us. So a day later there was a big firefight there and they [British troops] took them all out.

Another point noted by Marine Cole was that on occasions the firing from numerous GPMGs against the Argentine jets became a danger to those around the shore and on other ships,

by virtue of thousands of rounds of free-flying ammunition – thus ceasefire calls were frequent. Another Marine interviewed for this book, signaller Mark Crawford, also remembers incidents of spent Seacat missiles fired from the ships impacting around his position around Red Point House, near 3 Cdo HQ. He noted that luckily the ground around the shore was so soft that the Seacats penetrated deep into the earth, doing no significant damage and inflicting no friendly casualties.

Consolidation

With the Paras and Commandos ashore, and the beachhead secured, there now began the consolidation of the area. To ensure that the area was defendable, four batteries of 105mm guns (three from 29 Cdo Regt RA and one from the attached 4 Field Regt) were lifted ashore and set up, plus the Rapier batteries for air defence, although technical problems with those systems meant that they did not come online for several days. Three Blowpipe sections were deployed, these coming from the Air Defence Troops of 3 Commando Brigade HQ and Signals Squadron. One section went to Sussex Mountains, one to Ajax Bay and one to San Carlos Settlement.

There was also the need to build up the main logistics hub, known as the Brigade Maintenance Area (BMA), which was established at Ajax Bay. This was to be the nexus of constant logistical heli-lifts from the offshore vessels, with some 1,000 tonnes of supplies moved ashore in the first day alone. A major logistical problem, however, arose at the end of the first day, when the large ships *Canberra*, *Norland* and *Stromness* were ordered out of San Carlos Water because of the risk from air attacks. As Major General Kenneth L. Privratsky notes in his recommended reading *Logistics in the Falklands War*, this was a huge problem for the Commando Logistics Regiment because:

Their plans had hinged on LSLs and other ships anchored offshore to form a floating sustainment base within easy reach of the beachhead. . . . Canberra, for instance, was still carrying unit supplies and equipment for 40 Commando, 42 Commando, and 3 Para. Support echelons and first-line supplies for these units had not been transferred from Canberra to other vessels when combat units cross-decked at sea shortly before D-Day. Assault waves had taken only enough supplies to last forty-eight hours. Moreover, as they normally would when making an assault landing, the commandos and paratroopers had left rucksacks, parkas, sleeping gear, cooking items and extra clothes aboard troop transports. Some units, like 2 Para which disembarked from Norland, had not had the time to get personal gear to the beaches yet. If rucksacks and personal items did not get ashore, men would spend their first nights on land more uncomfortable than expected.[2]

ABOVE The logistics beachhead at San Carlos – a Mexeflote powered landing raft and an LCU deliver vehicles and stores. *(Defence Picture Library)*

ABOVE **A force protection team from 40 Cdo RM dig in at San Carlos; 40 Cdo was assigned to protect the rear of the British campaign.** *(Defence Picture Library)*

ABOVE RIGHT **A parting photograph looking up at** *Sir Galahad*, **while it was being abandoned on account of the unexploded bomb wedged below decks.** *(Andy Cole)*

BELOW **A blurred image of the hole punched through the side of** *Sir Galahad* **by the 1,000lb UXB dropped by a Skyhawk on 24 May.** *(Andy Cole)*

The only solution to the immediate problem was a Herculean and rapid effort, involving all manner of extra rotary assets brought in to heli-lift the supplies. Thereafter, the supplies were mainly transferred by LSLs, compelled to sail out to the distant vessels, which could be up to 200 miles (320km) away, and ferrying the materials back in – a process that was both slow and also stretched the offloading capacity of the logistics personnel to the maximum (by bringing back very large volumes of supplies at any one time). The BMA became a huge, and at times, chaotic location.

There was also the problem of getting the supplies out from the BMA to the troops inland, a task made seriously difficult by the lack of heavy helicopters to perform major airlifts; during the initial days of the landings, the commanders on shore were still waiting for the arrival of the Chinooks from *Atlantic Conveyor*, although these would all be lost on the sinking of 25 May. The very boggy terrain on the Falklands also made vehicle logistics problematic. The standard British Army Land Rover was often unable to traverse the terrain, especially if pulling a trailer with supplies. The most reliable means of moving gear overland was the tracked Bv 202. Note that a particular critical problem was how to get fuel moved forward, made particularly difficult by a general lack of jerrycans.

Yet the fact remained that though there were issues with supplies, the incredible ingenuity and efforts of Commando Logistics Regiment ensured that the British troops were still able to go forward and fight.

Battle of Darwin and Goose Green

The period between the landings at San Carlos on 21 May and 2 Para's famous attack on Darwin and Goose Green (26–28 May) was one of frustration, complications and friction at the higher levels of command. Thompson had received, on 12 May, a directive from Moore, at that point still sailing south with 5th Inf Bde and yet to take operational control of the land campaign. Part of the directive read:

You are to secure a bridgehead on East Falkland, into which reinforcements can be landed, in which an airstrip can be established and from which operations to repossess the Falklands can be achieved. You are to push forward from the bridgehead area, so far as the maintenance of security allows, to gain information, to establish moral and physical domination over the enemy and to forward the ultimate objective of repossession.

The job of establishing 'moral and physical domination over the enemy' was problematic, in terms of the evolving land campaign. The logistical hub needed to be built up to a level sufficient to support a major push forward, and this was not easy given the swarming air attacks over shipping in San Carlos Water and further afield. Then came the critical blow – the sinking of *Atlantic Conveyor*. At a stroke, Thompson lost most of his heavy air assault capability, with the destruction of the Chinooks and nine Wessex helicopters. This meant that if the Paras and Marines were to advance, they would have to go on foot, taking with them only the kit and equipment they could

physically carry, across exceptionally hard terrain, with all the implied time impositions and combat limitations. But on top of this, there was the pressure from the UK government to do something, to give the public a victory to balance out the loss of five ships so far.

ABOVE A Royal Marine radio operator serving with Air Defence Troop attached to 2 Para at Goose Green. *(Defence Picture Library)*

LEFT Lieutenant Colonel 'H' Jones, the commander of 2 Para, was awarded the posthumous Victoria Cross for his from-the-front leadership in the battle for Goose Green. *(Defence Picture Library)*

Thus it was that Thompson and his staff opted to assault the Argentine garrison at Darwin and Goose Green, using 2 Para under the command of Lieutenant Colonel 'H' Jones. The objective was indeed a logical next step. The Argentine position, set within a narrow neck of land, was just 15 miles (24km) south of the San Carlos landings, and therefore posed a genuine threat to the British foothold. Intelligence about the Argentine strength there was uncertain, and tended towards underestimation. The principal defensive formation was the 12th 'General Arenales' Infantry Regiment, designated as 'Task Force Mercedes' and commanded by Lieutenant General Ítalo Piaggi, with a strength of 643 men. (The commander of all the Darwin/Goose Green garrison was Wing Commander Wilson Pedrozo, with Piaggi in tactical control.) Half of the regiment consisted of new, bewildered and cold conscripts, but at least they had a tough and intelligent commander in Piaggi. His force was augmented by C Company, 25th Infantry Regiment, and a platoon from 8th Infantry Regiment, plus the ground troops within the Fuerza Aérea Argentina deployed to the air base in the south of the isthmus. Total Argentine ground troops were therefore about 1,000, although we must always bear in mind that the total forces available does not equate to the actual number of men fighting on the front line at any given time). In terms of heavy firepower, Piaggi could also draw upon a battery of 105mm guns and 20mm and 35mm AA guns of the 601st AA Battalion. With the guns in support around Goose Green, Piaggi's troops were in highly defensible positions across the full width of the isthmus further north, mainly concentrated along Darwin Ridge between Boca House to the west and the settlement of Darwin itself to the east.

Facing this tough obstacle were some 500 men of 2 Para. For local support fire they would carry with them GPMGs, MILANs and two 81mm mortars. In addition they would have artillery support from three airlifted 105mm guns of 8 Battery, 29 Cdo Regt RA, and air defence from RA and RM Blowpipe SAM detachments. HMS *Arrow* would provide offshore 4.5in NGS, and Harrier GR.3s were available for CAS from *Hermes*.

The basic plan was for 2 Para to march down to the start line around Burntside Pond, while the Support Company established a fire support base at Camilla Creek. The attack would be launched at night (H-Hour 02:00hrs) by four companies:

- A Coy (Major C.D. Farrar-Hockley)
- B Coy (Major J.H. Crosland)
- C Coy (Major R. Jenner)
- D Coy (Major P. Neame).

BELOW Map of the battle of Goose Green/ Darwin. *(Defence Picture Library)*

In rough outline, A Coy would assault the Argentine right wing, heading for Coronation Point via Burntside House. B Coy would take the opposite flank, striking towards Boca House, while D Coy would take the centre ground. C Coy and the Support Company would ultimately support the push through to Goose Green with D Coy; it was expected that Goose Green would be liberated by about 06:00hrs. In retrospect, given the strength of the defensive forces, the timing was optimistic. Also, just prior to the attack, in a terrible security lapse, the BBC effectively broadcast 2 Para's intention to assault Darwin and Goose Green. Thus the incredulous and anxious Argentines would be ready and waiting.

The battle for Darwin and Goose Green began on 28 May, on the back of an exhausting combat march down to the start line on 26–27th, the 105mm guns being lifted to Camilla Creek House by Sea Kings from No. 846 NAS. At 01:45hrs, *Arrow* began its NGS mission, although a technical problem with the gun would later result in broken fire support. A Coy began its assault against Burntside House at around 02:35hrs (some 30 minutes later than planned), but found almost no resistance – Burntside House proved to be occupied only by four civilians, who survived the heavy small-arms fire poured into their building. B Coy went forward about 30 minutes later, with D Coy and Tac HQ following, all with artillery support. Resistance stiffened here, an Argentine company putting out heavy fire despite being tactically outclassed. D Coy had a tough time dealing with two .50-cal machine guns on their right flank, and three Paras from that company were killed in just the first two hours of the action. The remnants of the Argentine company were eventually dislodged and pulled back to the main defence line, but they had succeeded in delaying the British advance.

Under Jones's tight direction – some would later say excessively tight – the attack inched forward, with A Coy moving past Coronation Point (the positions there were unoccupied) and pushing against the 100ft (32m) high Darwin Hill position while B Coy went up towards the Boca House defences on the right flank. Piaggi, rightly judging that the Darwin Ridge positions were critical to the Argentine defensive battle

plan, reinforced the line, with an 8th Infantry Regiment platoon sent to Boca Hill (with a commanding view of Boca House) and a platoon from 25th Infantry Regiment going up on the Darwin Ridge.

The fight to push through the main Argentine defences was brutal and confused, with intense close-quarters engagements taking place around numerous positions in either darkness or, as day broke, wet and foggy weather (which for a time precluded the Harrier CAS missions). Jones's timeline for the action was now in tatters, as the battle extended through the morning towards midday. Both sides were also taking heavy casualties, dead and wounded. For the Paras, the fatalities included, shockingly, Lieutenant Colonel Jones himself. Attempting to galvanise the stalled operation, Jones ran up a gulley at about 10:30hrs towards an Argentine position almost on his own, and was fatally wounded by a burst of small-arms fire. Major Chris Keeble thereafter took command of 2 Para, and set about reformulating the attack plan with his other company commanders.

Despite their exhaustion, the Paras were quickly learning what worked and what didn't at a tactical level. Clearing small positions, for example, was best achieved with a combination of both fragmentation and phosphorus grenades, thrown in that order. The MILAN was proving to be very useful for demolishing individual outposts. The need for heavy support fire was also clear; GPMGs were positioned in massed groups, pouring suppressive lethal torrents down on to the Argentines. Ammunition

ABOVE Wounded and battle-fatigued Argentine soldiers at Goose Green following the night battle; medics from the Paras treat some of the wounded with immediate first aid. *(Defence Picture Library)*

RIGHT A paratrooper
with an Argentine
prisoner. The prisoner
is wearing a jumper
taken from one of
the Royal Marines
captured at the
beginning of the war.
(Defence Picture Library)

BELOW Morning
breaks over the Goose
Green battlefield on
29 May, the Paras
having fought for the
entire previous day.
(Defence Picture Library)

BELOW RIGHT A
soldier from 2 Para
enjoys a well-earned
rest, brewing up some
tea in a canteen.
(Defence Picture Library)

expenditure, however, was worryingly high and supplies were running low by late morning.

Finally, the breakthrough came. While A Coy continued its assault on Darwin Hill, two platoons of D Coy made a wide flanking mission along the beach on the western side of the isthmus, an action that broke the impasse. Boca Hill was taken after heavy fighting, and the combined effort of B and D Coys finally suppressed Boca

House. By midday, the Darwin Ridge defences had been fractured, but also by this time the Paras were coming under air attack by Grupo 3 Pucarás, which were able to operate in poorer weather than the Harriers. The strafing attacks inflicted several casualties, although one of the aircraft was shot down by a Blowpipe.

The British offensive was now advancing on Goose Green, albeit against continuing heavy resistance and desperate exhaustion among the Paras. The Argentines had also received some reinforcements – around 80 men were heli'd in from Stanley to positions just south of Goose Green. Furthermore, during the afternoon the air attacks intensified with the addition of two MB-339 aircraft in the Argentine CAS role, and Pucarás even resorted to dropping napalm. Thankfully for the British, as the weather improved later in the afternoon, the GR.3s from *Hermes* were able to fly in and add their support, delivering rocket and CBU attacks (though one Harrier was shot down in the action). These air assaults were especially directed towards the Argentine air force 20mm and 35mm gun positions, which caused serious problems for the Paras as they moved up around Goose Green.

As the evening beckoned, it was a concerning time for the British, as there were still some 800 defenders who had been forced back into the Goose Green area. Thompson recognised that the battle hung in the balance, and placed J Coy, 42

RIGHT The cost – bodies of the 16 Paras killed during the battle are placed in temporary battlefield graves. *(Defence Picture Library)*

Cdo, on standby as a reinforcement. But over on the Argentine side, there was the recognition that the defence was futile. Goose Green was now cut off – the Para B Coy had swung deep to the south, trapping Goose Green between B Coy to the south and A and C Coys to the north and west. More reinforcements had been flown in, but it was obvious that continued action would lead to heavy loss of life, for uncertain gains. With hindsight, it is possible that the Argentines could have unleashed a counter-offensive against the Paras, with the possibility of success, but such can only be seen from the comfort of an armchair. As it was, Argentine negotiations for surrender began around 20:30hrs, and were completed during the early hours of the next day. The Paras had taken the first British land victory of the war.

It was a victory at cost, however. A total of 16 Paras had been killed and 33 wounded; Argentine casualties were 145 dead and wounded. What was clear was that Argentine troops, even ones with scarcely any training behind them, would not just fold up before the advance of the British. This was sobering information at the very beginning of the land forces campaign.

ABOVE Following the Goose Green/Darwin battle, soldiers of 2 Para wait to be airlifted forward to Fitzroy and Bluff Cove. *(Defence Picture Library)*

LEFT Soldiers of 2 Para wait to be airlifted forward, for once not having to rely upon leg power alone. *(Defence Picture Library)*

Chapter Seven

Land combat ops – the advance to Stanley

The battle of **Goose Green** and Darwin began the advance towards Stanley in earnest. In its broadest outlines, the British land campaign plan was to move out of the **San Carlos** bridgehead towards the Falklands capital on multiple lines of advance, with **3 Cdo** advancing on a northerly route and **5 Inf Bde** units, once they had arrived, taking a more southerly direction. The Argentine defences at Stanley would be progressively constricted, with their backs to the sea.

OPPOSITE Much of the British advance across the islands would be done on foot. Lower leg injuries – especially stress fractures and twisted ankles/knees – were commonplace. *(Defence Picture Library)*

139

RIGHT **A Marine tends to his feet; water seepage into the DMS boot was a major problem, resulting in many cases of trench foot.** *(Defence Picture Library)*

The land campaign would progressively focus on taking the key defensive points of high ground around Stanley, steadily shrinking the Argentine defensive perimeter. To ensure that the attacks had the immediate logistical support they needed, Forward Brigade Maintenance Areas (FBMAs) were to be established at Teal Inlet further to the west and Fitzroy, on the eastern coast. Given the Paras' experience at Darwin and Goose Green, there were no expectations that this would be an easy or straightforward campaign.

Moving forward and the arrival of 5 Bde

On Thursday 27 May, even as 2 Para fought for survival, 45 Cdo and 3 Para, the latter accompanied by 4 Troop of the Blues & Royals, began a long and physically punishing march across the northern parts of East Falkland, heading for Teal Inlet, an overland journey of some 32km (20 miles); Teal Inlet itself was about 37km (23 miles) from Stanley. The two formations took different routes, the Marines to the north via Douglas and the Paras the more southerly, and direct, of the two lines of advance. By Sunday 30 May, both

THE 'YOMP' TO TEAL INLET

The following account of the Marines' 'yomp' (or 'tab' to the Paras) across East Falkland, written by Captain Ian Gardiner, is a striking insight into the human toughness required for an operation largely without vehicular or rotary support:

The walk from Port San Carlos to New House, some twenty kilometres, was the worst of my life. The weather was not too bad but the ground was boggy, there were strong lumps and tufts of grass which, however one stands on them, even in daylight, one stands a good chance of turning one's ankle. In places it was pretty steep but all faded into insignificance compared to the cursed weight we were carrying – much of which I knew to be wholly unnecessary. I probably made things worse for myself by allowing my bitterness to burn up the energy – but the Marines were magnificent. We lost the first man after 200 yards – a man known to be the Company skate – and about six more over the next few hours. They were mostly the weaker-spirited men who, although they possibly did have something wrong with them, would probably have found some pretext or other to roll around in agony in any event. The rest went on with the greatest of stoicism and good humour all day and through until 2 o'clock the following morning. I am immensely proud of them. If possible, marching in darkness was worse than daylight, and, for those at the tail end of the queue of 600 men bumping and stumbling through the black night, life must have been hell. I was fairly preoccupied by trying to keep people together and perhaps didn't notice so much, but by the time we leaguered up, I was near my wit's end.

formations had reached Teal Inlet but then split, with 3 Para plus the Scimitars heading out to occupy Mount Estancia, while 45 Commando remained at Teal Inlet.

Another crucial and opportunistic deployment took place from Friday 28 May, when 42 Cdo began occupying Mount Kent, just over 8km (5 miles) from Stanley. (Note that 40 Cdo would remain around San Carlos for the rest of the campaign as a rearguard defence force.) Mount Kent had already been occupied in part by the SAS, and the hill's proximity to Stanley meant that it was the ideal location to set up a forward artillery base. On 28 May, the K Coy, 42 Cdo, was flown in to occupy Mount Kent's summit in two Sea Kings, joined shortly after by a battery of 105mm guns (7 Bty RA), courtesy of the only Chinook flying in the theatre. Occupying the exposed position atop Mount Kent was not the most exciting, or comfortable posting, for the Marines, but it was an important one, and the gun battery was able to bring down its first rounds on Stanley on 1 June. L Coy joined the Mount Kent position temporarily before marching out to occupy Mount Challenger, which it came to share with J Coy.

As an aside to the Marine and Para advance, a short and decisive engagement took place at Top Malo House, a solitary and abandoned shepherd's house just south of Teal Inlet. A four-man patrol group from the Mountain & Arctic Warfare Cadre (M&AWC) spotted the deployment by helicopter of 17 Argentine soldiers, who took up occupation of the house. In response, the commander of the M&AWC, Captain Rod Boswell, put together a force of 19 men and helicoptered them in on 31 May to conduct an assault, the helicopter winding its way at ultra-low level through the valleys and along rivers. An intense close-quarters firefight took place, in which five of the Argentines were killed and the remainder captured; three Marines were wounded.

On 1 June, the nature of the British land campaign in the Falklands shifted, as 5 Inf Bde began to arrive in San Carlos Water. The

RIGHT SBS soldiers prepare to deploy from the exit chamber of a submarine. *(Defence Picture Library)*

ABOVE Marines snake in single column across the Falkland Islands on their way to Stanley. The total distance between San Carlos and Stanley is about 45 miles (74km), as the crow flies. *(Defence Picture Library)*

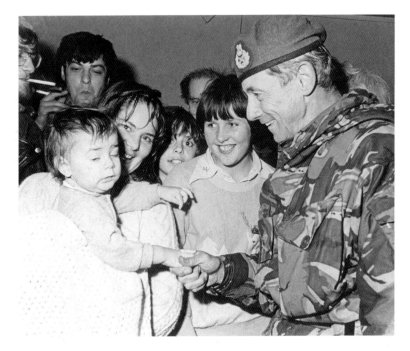

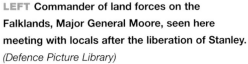

LEFT **Commander of land forces on the Falklands, Major General Moore, seen here meeting with locals after the liberation of Stanley.** *(Defence Picture Library)*

change in the theatre was profound, with both positive and some negative implications. There was a command reconfiguration, as Moore took overall command of the land forces while Thompson concentrated solely on 3 Cdo Bde operations. The 5 Inf Bde deployment brought in substantial forces, specifically:

- 1st Welsh Guards
- 2nd Scots Guards
- 1/7th Gurkha Rifles
- 4 Field Regiment RA
- 36 Engineer Regiment RE
- No. 656 AAC Squadron.

Furthermore, Moore redistributed some of the forces already on the Falklands. The biggest shifts were the transfer to 5 Bde control of 2 Para, 40 Cdo, 29 Bty RA and the Blues & Royals.

The most significant problem generated by the deployment of 5 Bde was logistical. Keeping the war effort supplied fell yet again upon the sagging shoulders of the Commando Logistics Regiment, which was now critically overstretched serving a force many times larger than that for which it was designed. Furthermore, the dramatic expansion of the number of personnel at the San Carlos bridgehead raised the question of how they would be deployed around Stanley. Although the Paras and Marines had marched to their objectives, this situation was not ideal, and not suited to all formations. The 5 Bde shipping did bring in more helicopter resources, but not sufficient for an airlift movement of all troops.

A breakthrough to this problem came on 3 June. Through a fortunate telephone

LEFT In this famous image, RM Corporal Peter Robinson marches across the Falklands with the Union flag on his backpack. *(Defence Picture Library)*

conversation between Colour Sergeant Morris of 2 Para and islander Roy Binney at Swan Inlet, on the approaches to Fitzroy, it was ascertained that the anchorages at both Fitzroy and Bluff Cove, both just to the south of Stanley, were free from Argentines. Pouncing on this information, the commander of 5 Bde, Brigadier Tony Wilson, ordered the rapid heliborne deployment of 2 Para from Goose Green to Fitzroy and Bluff Cove, securing two forward outposts. To capitalise on this gain, Moore then decided to deploy both of the Guards regiments to these positions using the LCUs *Intrepid* and *Fearless*.

On 5 and 6 June, the Scots Guards and the HQ and 2 Coy of the 1st Welsh Guards were moved forward to Bluff Cove. It was then felt that making the LCUs do the journey again was too risky, hence the LSLs *Sir Tristram* and *Sir Galahad* were tasked with moving more supplies and men on 7–8 June; the remainder of the Welsh Guards would be embarked aboard *Sir Galahad*.

By this time in the campaign, *Sir Galahad* had already been on the receiving end of Argentine air attacks. On 24 May, the ship had been hit by a 1,000lb (454kg) Argentine bomb, which fortunately did not explode; the ship was evacuated while EOD experts defused the threat. But on 8 June in Fitzroy (coastal conditions meant that *Sir Galahad* had to divert

to Fitzroy, rather than the intended Bluff Cove), her luck ran out in dreadful fashion. During an air attack in the early afternoon, the ship was hit by multiple bombs, and was engulfed in flames. Horrifically, the vessel was still packed with its human cargo, there having been delays in deploying the Welsh Guards to shore. In the disaster that unfolded, 48 people were killed, including 32 of the Guardsmen, with dozens wounded; combined with the loss of stores, it delivered a critical blow to the battalion's combat capability. *Sir Tristram* was also hit by bombs, set on fire and destroyed, but thankfully the casualty count was far lower – two men killed. It was a salutary reminder that the war could still hang in the balance, even as the British closed in on Stanley.

The plan of attack

By 10 June 1982, Argentine forces on the Falklands occupied a series of defensive positions on the approaches to, and within, Stanley. Even with the deployment of 5 Bde forces south of Stanley, there was no real way to take the capital except by a conventional infantry advance from west to east.

The plan for the offensive was basically broken down into three phases, each phase based on taking roughly concentric and shrinking defensive lines:

ABOVE The rescue effort at Bluff Cove saw Sea King helicopters repeatedly fly into the flames and smoke of the burning ships, often at great risk to themselves from exploding ordnance. Here helicopters swarm around *Sir Galahad*, from which rescued crewmen are rowed to shore. *(Defence Picture Library)*

Phase 1

Main British unit	Objective(s)	Main Argentine defenders
3 Para	Mount Longdon	7th Inf Regt
45 Cdo	Two Sisters and possible attack on Mount Tumbledown	4th Inf Regt
42 Cdo (plus supporting elements from Welsh Guards and 40 Cdo)	Mount Harriet, plus possibility of diverting to support 45 Cdo	4th Inf Regt

Phase 2

Main British unit	Objective(s)	Main Argentine defenders
2nd Scots Guards and 1/7th Gurkha Rifles	Mount Tumbledown and Mount William	5th Marine Infantry Battalion
2 Para and Blues & Royals	Wireless Ridge	7th Inf Regt

Phase 3

Main British unit	Objective(s)	Main Argentine defenders
5 Inf Bde	Sapper Hill	5th Marine Infantry Battalion
3 Cdo Bde		Multiple elements, including 5th Marine Infantry Battalion 3rd Inf Regt 6th Inf Regt 7th Inf Regt 25th Inf Regt

Phase 1 of the operation, for what was labelled the Outer Defence Zones, was scheduled for 11/12 June. It promised to be hard going, as the positions held by the Argentines were complex, often difficult to spot, and protected by copious support fire, plus in some positions minefields. But there were factors that favoured the British. The first was that since the occupation of the forward hills, the British had been able to observe and pinpoint more accurately the Argentine locations, which therefore became the regular recipients of preparatory NGS, artillery fire and Harrier ground-attack missions. Also, the Argentine commander on the Falklands, General Menéndez, had plenty of troops at his disposal, but the possibility of a further sudden British amphibious action around Stanley meant that he had to keep many of them tied to coastal defence. Furthermore, although the Argentine regiments and battalions did include some excellent troops, including the marines, many of

LEFT A Royal Marine sniper team (armed with L42A1 rifle), apply camouflage prior to operations.
(Defence Picture Library)

the men were cold, frightened, demoralised and poorly led.

In the accounts that follow, I have separated the individual battles out for clarity, although it is worth remembering that many of them took place simultaneously in what must have been nights of tremendous drama and violence.

The battle of Mount Longdon (11/12 June)

Mount Longdon was a critical feature in the Argentine defence. The mountain (or more accurately, hill) was dominated by a long ridgeline 600ft (180m) above the ground. The terrain was rocky and complicated, which aided the defenders. The defences on Longdon included multiple 7.62mm and .50-cal machine-gun positions, 120mm mortar support, 105mm recoilless rifles, anti-tank missiles and night-vision equipped snipers from the 501 Company of Argentine SF. The British 3 Para, commanded by Lieutenant Colonel H.W.R. Pike, was also heavily armed internally, plus had the fire support of six 105mm guns from 79 Bty, 29 Cdo Regt RA, plus the 4.5in gun of the Type 21 frigate HMS *Avenger*. Nevertheless, it was clear that a hard fight lay ahead.

The plan was for A and B Coys to make the attack, with C Coy in reserve. The attack would go in from the west, with B Coy (4, 5, 6 Platoons) to clear the ridge in a south-westerly direction, taking the features nicknamed, according to rugby terminology, 'Fly Half' and 'Full Back'. A Coy (1, 2, 3 Platoons) would take the more northerly feature known as 'Wing Forward', which it would turn into a fire support base to assist B Coy movement. If all went to plan, A and C Coys could also then divert to assault nearby Wireless Ridge to the east.

From its launch at 21:00hrs, however, the operation went awry. On the approach to Longdon, a 4 Coy soldier trod on a mine, triggering a blazing response fire from the Argentine positions, the defenders firing from advantageous elevation. Through heavy small-arms and mortar fire, the Paras pushed up on to the ridge, with 6 Platoon managing to drive ahead and take 'Fly Half'. But the B Coy attack subsequently stalled under appalling fire. Enemy positions were taken out with MILANs and LAWs,

but the Paras were also taking heavy casualties, including 4 Pltn's Sergeant Ian McKay, who was subsequently awarded the posthumous Victoria Cross (VC) for his leadership in taking out an Argentine .50-cal position. But such was the intensity of the resistance that 4 and 5 Pltns were pulled back. British 105mm artillery fire and offshore naval bombardment worked hard to try to reduce the Argentine defence further. One Argentine soldier remembered:

It was hell, bombs were falling on all sides, but we were lucky, we weren't hit. An NCO was in charge of the gun [a 105mm gun], but an ordinary soldier lined it up, an absolute phenomenon, he shot very accurately. Over the radio, from a hill on the frontline, the orders came: 'Shoot again, number three gun, shoot again, hitting the area well. . . .' But when the British realised that the gun was causing them trouble, they began to hunt it down. They had equipment which detected any kind of gunfire, even rifle shots, marking the exact coordinates of its position. Their artillery then began to aim for the troublespot. . . . The bombs became more and more frequent, about one every two seconds. They were destroying all the mortars they detected. It was amazing. We must have fired 20 rounds at them with the field gun and they fired 100 at us.[2]

ABOVE The morning after the battle of Mount Longdon, Paras display a regimental flag in celebration at the victory. (*Defence Picture Library*)

and southern, with a 'saddle' in between. Occupying defensive positions along its entire length was the Argentine 4th Infantry Regiment, commanded by Major Ricardo Cordón. Its 1st and 2nd Platoons, C Company, occupied the northern peak, while the company's 3rd Platoon was on the southern peak. In between was the 1st Platoon, A Company, and a Support Platoon, while further to the east was B Company of the 6th Regiment in reserve.

Taking Two Sisters would be the responsibility of 45 Cdo, commanded by Lieutenant Colonel A.F. Whitehead, with D-Day set for the night of 11/12 June, in sympathy with the other attacks on the outer Argentine defences. In the week leading up to the assault, 45 Cdo advanced cautiously out from Mount Kent to their start positions, a movement that in itself brought localised and vicious clashes with Argentine troops. One of these, an engagement between Lieutenant Chris Fox's Recon Troop and an Argentine patrol, developed into a major firefight that resulted in 12 Argentine soldiers killed; the Marines suffered no casualties. But there were also losses for the Marines on the advance. On the night of 9 June, five Marines died and two were wounded when the Marines' own mortar troop fired on one of their patrols, confusing them for Argentine soldiers in the darkness. It was the worst of several 'blue-on-blue' incidents during the war.

Nevertheless, 45 Cdo eventually reached its start lines for the operation, with Y and Z Coy at 'Pub Garden' located just to the north-west of Two Sisters, while X Coy was to the south-west. (The battle-worn 2 Para was in reserve.) The plan was for X Coy to begin its assault at 21:00hrs directly towards the southern peak, which had an elevation of 1,070ft (326m). The approach would begin silently, but once battle was drawn 45 Cdo could count on the assistance of six 105mm guns of 8 Bty, 29 Cdo Regt RA, plus the twin 4.5in guns of HMS *Glamorgan* offshore. The aim was to clear the peak, codename 'Long Toenail', and establish a fire support base that could be used to suppress Argentine defences on the northern peak (codename 'Summer Days') that would be assaulted by Y and Z Coys. Z Coy would take 'Summer Days' directly, while Y Coy cleared positions just to the east.

A Coy, meanwhile, was also having an appalling close-combat experience as it pushed towards the 'Wing Forward' position. It became clear that a forward advance was not going to be possible so, adapting to the situation, A Coy swung back to the western edge of Longdon and now began the push along the ridgeline originally attempted by B Coy. This time, the advance made brutal passage along the full length of the ridge, eventually reaching 'Full Back' as the Argentine resistance finally collapsed.

By daybreak, Mount Longdon was in 3 Para's hands, but at the cost of 23 dead and 43 wounded. Exact Argentine casualties are unknown, possibly about 50 killed and 123 wounded. Further punishment for 3 Para came in the form of long-range artillery fire, which struck their positions on Longdon for the next two days.

The battle of Two Sisters (11/12 June)

Located to the south-west of Longdon, Two Sisters sat roughly equidistant between Mount Kent and Mount Tumbledown, and was aligned on a direct west–east axis with Stanley itself. This geographical feature – as its name implies – consists of two peaks, northern

The operation to clear Two Sisters began two hours late, the Marines struggling under their burdens of equipment to make the start lines. But at 23:00hrs X Coy began to go forward, led by Captain Ian Gardiner. After covering about 1km (0.6 miles) distance, the company's covert deployment was eventually blown, and the whole night-time landscape erupted in blistering fire and counterfire, the darkness split by thousands of tracer rounds and the detonations of grenades, mortar rounds, artillery shells and missiles. The level of resistance was breathtaking, and although some of the Marine troops managed to ascend to near the summit, the Argentine 105mm and 155mm artillery and machine-gun fire eventually forced them back and the X Coy attack began to stall.

Seeing the blockage, Whitehead now decided to deploy his Y and Z Coys before 'Long Toenail' was cleared. Their approach had the advantage of the distraction coming from the battle for the neighbouring peak, but eventually too, the silent approach turned into a very heavy firefight, four Marines quickly becoming fatal casualties. The Marine 8 Troop gained the momentum when they stormed to near the peak of 'Summer Days', clearing the Argentine positions one at a time with small

arms, grenades and the ever-useful MILAN, each shot costing £10,000. Y Coy was also coming forward, swinging south and then east of Z Coy's attack, and suppressing some key Argentine defences in the process. With Y Coy relieving some of the pressure on Z Coy, the latter was then able to take the summit.

Although Argentine artillery would keep coming in, and did so well after the battle, the resistance on Two Sisters was now crumbling, with white flags appearing by dawn, when the objective was finally secured.

Incredibly, given the awesome level of firepower directed at Two Sisters, there were only eight British fatalities (seven Marines and an Army engineer), plus 17 wounded. Total Argentine casualties numbered 124, including 50 taken prisoner. When observing the strength of the Argentine defensive positions, Whitehead famously remarked: 'Give me 120 men and I could die of old age defending this hill.' The victory on Two Sisters, a highly defensible position, was an indication that the Argentine resistance was beginning to disintegrate. This being said, it had by no means been a walkover. One Marine remarked in a note: 'I am still trying to forget that night, so I will write no more about it.'

ABOVE Marines oversee the surrender of ammunition (largely piles of FN magazines) and equipment held by Argentine forces. *(Defence Picture Library)*

Battle of Mount Harriet (11/12 June)

While 45 Cdo wrested Two Sisters from the Argentine grip, 42 Cdo (commander Lieutenant Colonel Nick Vaux) was doing likewise on Mount Harriet, 3km (2 miles) to the south-east. Once again, it was the Argentine 4th Infantry Regiment that took the main defensive role in this sector, although it was supported by elements of the 1st 'Patricios' Infantry Regiment, the Regiment of Mounted Grenadiers and 17th Airborne Infantry Regiment. The Mount Harriet position also had extensive minefield defences on its approaches.

As the battle of Two Sisters would be taking place such a short distance to the north, Vaux opted for a two-pronged approach that would steer well clear of the other attack. He decided to keep J Coy deployed on Wall Mountain, just a mile to the west of Mount Harriet, and from there to provide diversionary fire. (The 1st Welsh Guards and A and C Coys, 40 Cdo, were to act as the reserve.) The actual assault on Mount Harriet would be carried out by K (1, 2, 3 Troops) and L Coy (4, 5, 6 Troops). Together they would make a long, wide approach to the south, eventually swinging north to attack Mount Harriet from the south-east, with K Coy moving along the eastern half of the feature, and L Coy the western half. In support would be the six 105mm guns of 7 Bty, 29 Cdo Regt RA, plus the 4.5in guns of HMS *Yarmouth*, and also 42 Cdo's own 81mm mortars.

The key to the attack would be for K and L Coys to get as close as possible to their objective before being detected. Vaux gave the instruction:

Surprise and absolute silence are vital. If necessary, you must go through the old business of making every man jump up and down before he starts, to check that nothing rattles. Persistent coughers must be left behind. If you find yourself in a minefield, remember that you must go on. [. . .] The enemy are very well dug-in in very strong positions. But I believe that, once we get in among them, they will crack pretty quickly.

The southerly advance began in the early hours of darkness, with K and L Coys reaching their start line positions around 22:00hrs, having

RIGHT Marines of 42 Cdo take a break from operations, fatigue clearly etched on their faces. *(Defence Picture Library)*

negotiated a minefield. Moving out from the start line up Mount Harriet, K Coy managed to advance to within about 100yd (90m) of the Argentine defences before they were detected and battle began. On the eastern side of the summit, K Coy made tough but steady progress up the hill. As with the battle for Two Sisters, the support fire made the night battle an explosive and terrifying experience, with the British artillery firing constant 'danger close' missions just 55yd (50m) in front of the Marines (a total of 3,000 rounds would be hammered into Mount Harriet during the battle). Adding to the horror was the continual return fire of the Argentine guns. One of the biggest problems for the Marines was machine-gun bunkers, and many of the six gallantry awards given that night (four Military Medals, one Military Cross and a DSO) were granted for tackling such lethal obstacles.

To the west, L Coy was also grinding its way through the Argentine defences under intense fire. It took its half of the summit just before dawn, as did K Coy, which then pushed on off Mount Harriet towards a position further north known as 'Goat Ridge'. At daybreak, J Coy was also committed to the battle, moving

forward from Wall Mountain to assist the other two companies in clearing Mount Harriet.

By 09:00hrs, 42 Cdo had essentially won, and Mount Harriet was in British hands. Astonishingly, the Marines had taken only one fatality, a testament to excellent planning, preparation and training. The Argentines, meanwhile, had lost yet another position on the approaches to Stanley, plus 300 of their soldiers went into captivity.

ABOVE The LSL *Sir Galahad* on fire off Fitzroy after being hit by an Argentine bomb strike. The *Galahad* had the Welsh Guards aboard, who had been waiting for orders to move off the ship. *(Defence Picture Library)*

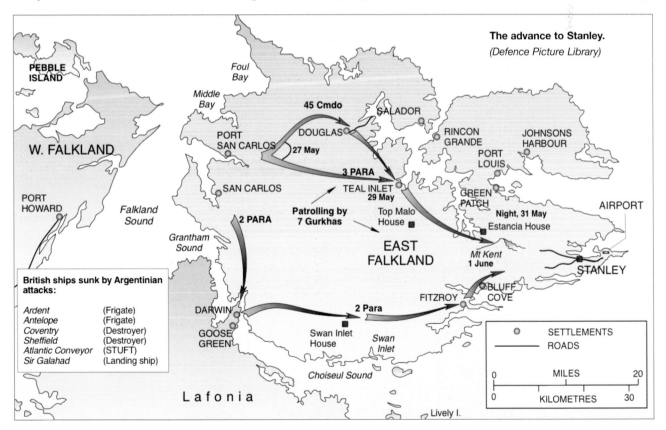

The advance to Stanley. *(Defence Picture Library)*

British ships sunk by Argentinian attacks:

Ardent	(Frigate)
Antelope	(Frigate)
Coventry	(Destroyer)
Sheffield	(Destroyer)
Atlantic Conveyor	(STUFT)
Sir Galahad	(Landing ship)

SBS member 'Baz' was involved in numerous small-scale engagements – including some hand-to-hand fighting – with Argentine forces as his team roamed across the islands. Here he gives his general impression of the quality of the enemy when faced with the SF soldiers, and also explains some of the SBS tactics used:

They were good fighters, but they were predictable . . . and we weren't predictable, I suppose that's what made us different, we didn't follow the rule book. Their responses would be predictable. We could say that if we were going to attack, then this is what they would do, and they did. They would set up a forward firing range, they would set up a forward mortar range, they would try to flank. Running a simple ellipse . . . they hadn't thought of that. They didn't think of how we would react. We were able to watch them attacking where we had been. We used to do the hit-and-run tactics, and they would implode upon the area where we had been. A couple of times we were a little sloppy and didn't get out as fast as we liked, but that's the way it goes. But we were also able to start identifying and picking off their leaders. I [would] put two men forward, get them as close as we could, to try to identify their leaders, what they were doing etc., and then get back to me. Then we would have a quick conflab . . . and then we'd take them out. More often than not we'd go in close to do it, and then get out, because they weren't expecting that – 10 yards away, Bang! Bang! Bang! Gone. Use the weather for cover. Your escape is the first 5 to 10 yards – if you can escape 5 to 10 yards then you've done it, because out there your visibility is so low.

BELOW Argentine prisoners under escort at a Forward Air Refuelling Point (FARP). *(Defence Picture Library)*

The battle for Wireless Ridge (13/14 June)

The three battles of 11/12 June had been critical victories on the way to Stanley, and had caused panic and a collapse in morale in both the Argentine high command and among its soldiery. Yet for the British, this was no time for complacency. Menéndez still had substantial forces held back in Stanley, and there was always the possibility of a counter-attack against an open British flank. Thus momentum had to be maintained.

The night of 13/14 June saw two of the last major land engagements of the war, those fought at Wireless Ridge and Mount Tumbledown plus the British advance in the south to Mount William and Sapper Hill. Once all these features were locked in British hands, then the Argentines would essentially be trapped around Stanley, held in place by British land forces to the west and the naval strength of the Task Force offshore around all other points of the compass.

In addition to the 7th Infantry Regiment, the Argentine defenders on Wireless Ridge also included soldiers from the 1st Argentine Parachute Regiment. The British attack was to be performed by 2 Para (commander: Lieutenant Colonel D.R. Chaundler), despite the fact of its punishing experience at Darwin/Goose Green just days earlier. (Note that for the Wireless Ridge operation 2 Para was moved back under the command of 3 Cdo Bde.) Yet the Paras now fully understood the importance of support fire, so they not only brought with them as many GPMGs, MILANs, LAWs and mortars as they could, they also had fire support from:

■ 3 Troop, Blues & Royals (2 × Scimitars; 2 × Scorpions)
■ 7 and 8 Btys, 29 Cdo Regt RA (12 × 105mm Light Guns)
■ 3 Para mortar support
■ NGS from HMS *Ambuscade* (1 × 4.5in gun) and HMS *Yarmouth* (2 × 4.5in guns).

Add the fact that during the battle two air strikes were carried out – SS.11 missiles were fired from Scout helicopters – then the battle of Wireless Ridge was a genuine 'all-arms' battle.

ABOVE **An SF sniper team, one (right) armed with a 7.62mm L41A1, the other with a 5.56mm M16 fitted with a Starlight scope.** *(Defence Picture Library)*

On the morning of 13 June, 2 Para moved up to what would be its start line for the attack, taking up a long, linear position along Furze Bush Pass, directly to the north of Wireless Ridge. Wireless Ridge itself had a summit of about 300ft (91m) elevation, running on an east–west axis, with its eastern end, crucially, sitting about a quarter of a mile north of Moody Brook Barracks, Stanley Harbour in clear sight. The north-to-south approach by the Paras would take them across several other elevated features. D Coy was to attack and secure 'Rough Diamond' to the north-east of Mount Longdon, after which it would advance south and then east, clearing the entire length of Wireless Ridge ('Blueberry Pie') in the process. A and B Coys, meanwhile, were to clear 'Apple Pie' – a piece of high ground on the left flank of the D Coy attack; once they had taken this feature, they would be able to deliver support fire to the D Coy advance along Wireless Ridge. The final element of the plan was a later attack by C Coy, which would move along the coastline on the left flank of A Coy (the most easterly of the 'Apple Pie' assaults), to attack and occupy a salient feature there.

The battle for Wireless Ridge was to be a 'noisy' attack, with heavy preliminary bombardment. The shelling of 'Rough Diamond' began shortly after midnight on 14 June, the

RIGHT A British
sniper, armed with
a 7.62mm L42A1
rifle, guards a line of
demoralised-looking
Argentine prisoners.
(Defence Picture Library)

BELOW Men of 2 Para
move into Stanley, the
town clearly having
suffered some battle
damage. *(Defence
Picture Library)*

105mm guns and the NGS hitting the Argentine positions hard (a total of 6,000 rounds were fired on to and around Wireless Ridge during the night). D Coy set out on its advance 30 minutes after the opening of the bombardment. Although the advance was made dangerous by Argentine 155mm artillery fire, including air-burst munitions, the Paras actually found 'Rough Diamond' largely abandoned, such had been the efficacy of the opening shelling.

A and B Coys were also now going forward, with the support of the Scimitars and Scorpions. The light armour of the Blues & Royals came into its own at Wireless Ridge. In particular, it was found especially useful for destroying stubborn Argentine gun positions, first by breaking apart the position with the main gun, then engaging those flushed out with the co-axial machine gun. As with D Coy, A and B Coys went ahead with little infantry resistance – again the demoralised defenders had often fled their posts – but the 155mm fire did inflict some casualties on the British. C Coy, rounding the bay above Wireless Ridge, also found the enemy positions largely deserted.

With 'Apple Pie' secure, A and C Coys were able to set up a firebase to support D Coy, which was now pushing from west to east along Wireless Ridge itself. The Argentine resistance stiffened on the eastern half of the ridge, but the combination of well-coordinated support fire and the accurate contributions of the armour vehicles, plus the Paras' own tactical skills, broke the Argentine defence and Wireless Ridge was in British hands by dawn. A localised platoon-strength counter-attack by Argentine troops was smashed up with little difficulty.

The battle for Wireless Ridge was now over,

apart from the occasional crash of enemy 155mm shells from Stanley. The Paras had lost three men killed and 11 injured, but the effects of the combined-arms firepower on the Argentines was devastating – more than 100 men had been killed. The engagement was clearly a turning point, and soldiers atop Wireless Ridge could clearly see the Argentine forces retreating back into Stanley.

Battle of Mount Tumbledown (13/14 June)

The battle of Mount Tumbledown was, alongside the clash at Wireless Ridge, essentially the last major land battle of the Falklands War. Unlike the other battles, which were almost exclusively the responsibilities of either Paras or Marines, on Tumbledown it was a 5 Inf Bde unit that now took the lead – 2nd Scots Guards.

Tumbledown was directly to the west of Stanley, a geographical feature some 2,000yd (1,828m) long and reaching a peak elevation of 800ft (243m). It was defended by one of the best of the Argentine units – the 5th Marine Infantry Brigade – with attached artillery and engineer support. Alongside Wireless Ridge, it was one of the last defensive outposts for the

Argentines – if it fell, then there would be no remaining elevated defences in front of Stanley.

The 2nd Scots Guards, led by Lieutenant Colonel Mike Scott, was – like the 2 Para attack on Wireless Ridge – bolstered by extremely heavy support forces. These included an impressive six batteries of 105mm guns, two Scimitars and two Scorpions from the Blues & Royals, mortar support from elements of 42 Cdo, the 1/7th Gurkha Rifles (who were also intended for an advance on nearby Mount William), plus NGS from the frigates *Active* and *Avenger*. In contrast to the Wireless Ridge battleplan, however, the Tumbledown operation would begin with a silent approach, moving in from the west along Goat Ridge then splitting into three company-strength assaults for the actual attack. G Coy (7, 8, 9 Pltns) would ascend the western part of the mountain; LF Coy (13, 14, 15 Pltns) would move through G Coy and take the central parts; RF Coy (1, 2, 3 Pltns) was tasked with occupying the easternmost defences. A diversionary attack would take place on the Fitzroy/Stanley track just before H-Hour to distract the Argentine defenders. (Note that 'LF' and 'RF' stand for 'Left Flank' and 'Right Flank' respectively.)

The diversionary attack began at 20:30hrs and was a substantial affair, including armour

ABOVE **Soldiers of the Scots Guards cheer after their hard-won victory on Mount Tumbledown.** *(Defence Picture Library)*

from the Blues & Royals. The British infantry element consisted of three four-man sections from the Recce Platoon plus a fire-support element. The diversion devolved into a two-hour battle that cost the British two dead, but the Argentines were certainly engrossed in its outcome as G Coy began its 1.9-mile (3km) advance out from its start line, the other two companies following close by. G Coy actually managed to secure its objectives with little

resistance, apart from long-range artillery fire, as many of the Argentines had already left their posts. The experience of LF Coy, however, was far more in keeping with the previous battles. Argentine resistance was trenchant, the marines obstinately holding on to every sangar and rocky outcrop. The 13 and 14 Pltns in particular were taking heavy casualties, the usual combination of AT rockets and grenades failing to quash the return fire. In the end, in what amounted to a seven-hour battle for the two platoons, bayonet charges and hand-to-hand fighting were the only solution to wresting control of several hard-held positions. By the time LF Coy finally took its objectives (HQ Coy also joined the fight in support), it had lost 7 dead and 18 wounded.

Now it was left to RF Coy to take the final parts of Tumbledown. Daybreak was approaching as the attack went in at 06:00hrs. Again, the Argentine marines showed their courage and resilience, and they had to be flushed out at close quarters with all the firepower the Scots Guards could muster. It took two solid hours of fighting before the Scots Guards could finally declare that all of Mount Tumbledown was in their hands.

Final surrender

With the collapse of Argentine resistance on Wireless Ridge, there was little now to prevent the British making the final assault on Stanley. The Gurkhas were sent forward to take Mount William, and the Welsh Guards Sapper Hill, but apart from some brief firefights these objectives were secured without incident – it had been a frustrating war for both the Gurkhas and the Welsh Guards. Now all that remained was the capital itself.

Menéndez still had some significant forces in the Stanley area – 8,000 troops in total – and was also under pressure from the junta back in Buenos Aires to keep resisting; they were sensing as much a political as a military disaster on the horizon. But the options for resistance were limited, especially as the Argentine forces had lost command of the sea some weeks ago and had now virtually surrendered the skies as well – both of these factors meant that there could be no relief or reinforcements from the mainland. The

RIGHT Major Rod Bell, the Royal Marine Spanish-speaking officer, carried out the surrender negotiations with Argentine commanders in Stanley at the end of the war. The Argentine leadership was a mixed bunch, all hamstrung by poor strategic handling of the war by the junta and by the high proportion of inexperienced conscripts under their command. *(Defence Picture Library)*

best defence that Menéndez could mount was essentially a siege ending in defeat, with heavy losses of life. Both 5 Bde and 3 Cdo were now bearing down on Stanley, and in the capital itself there was much chaos, soldiers milling about the streets in dense throngs of disorder. They, above all, did not want to die mounting a futile last stand for an outcrop of land for which most had no commitment or affinity.

As 2 Para entered the outskirts of Stanley, the two sides made contact and surrender negotiations began. Military advances and operations stopped while these were under way. Finally, terms were agreed and Menéndez signed an official instrument of surrender. The Falklands War, a conflict that began with seemingly all the cards stacked in Argentina's favour, had actually become one of the British armed forces' seminal victories.

LEFT A Marine guarding Argentine prisoners gives one POW what appears to be a very direct instruction. *(Defence Picture Library)*

INSTRUMENT OF SURRENDER

I, the undersigned, Commander of all the Argentine land, sea and air forces in the Falkland Islands surrender to Major General J.J. MOORE CB OBE MC* as representative of Her Britannic Majesty's Government.

Under the terms of this surrender all Argentine personnel in the Falkland Islands are to muster at assembly points which will be nominated by General Moore and hand over their arms, ammunition, and all other weapons and warlike equipment as directed by General Moore or appropriate British officers acting on his behalf.

Following the surrender all personnel of the Argentinian Forces will be treated with honour in accordance with the conditions set out in the Geneva Convention of 1949. They will obey any directions concerning movement and in connection with accommodation.

This surrender is to be effective from **2359** hours ZULU on **14** June (**2059** hours local) and includes those Argentine Forces presently deployed in and around Port Stanley, those others on East Falkland **[Menéndez's signature]**, West Falkland and all outlying islands.

[Menéndez's signature]
Commander Argentine Forces
[Moore's signature]
J.J. MOORE Major General
[Pennicott's signature]
Witness
2359 hours **14** June 1982

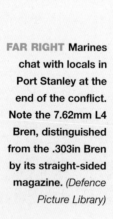

ABOVE A Scimitar of the Blues & Royals rumbles through the streets of Port Stanley at the end of the campaign. *(Defence Picture Library)*

BELOW An aerial view of sheds used as temporary homes for Argentine prisoners. *(Defence Picture Library)*

BELOW SS *Canberra* returns home after one of the most unexpected interludes of her maritime career. *(Defence Picture Library)*

Chapter Eight

Medical services

What had begun as a minor skirmish in a far corner of the South Atlantic evolved into a major regional conflict with a heavy loss of life. The final casualty toll by the end of the Falklands War was sobering – 255 British servicemen and 649 Argentines killed. In addition, 777 British troops were wounded, as were 1,188 Argentines. The word 'wounded' covers a broad spectrum of physical injury, ranging from a relatively minor laceration, repaired with a basic clean dressing, or perhaps a few stitches, through to limb amputations or whole-body burns, requiring major surgical intervention.

OPPOSITE In this revealing photograph, wounded have been transported to a CASEVAC point by Bv 202 vehicles, then lifted from the back into a waiting Scout helicopter. *(Defence Picture Library)*

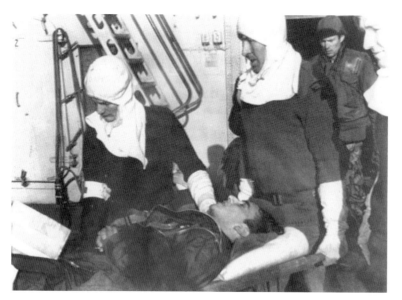

a staging post for serious casualty evacuation between the Falkland Islands and Ascension Island, as part of the transit route back to the UK, but the medical assistance offered there was limited for political reasons. So it was that the British medical teams had to rely as much on ingenuity, improvisation and professional talent to deliver a major package of care in the South Atlantic. As a point of note, it should also always be remembered that 30% of the entire casualties treated by the British medical staff were Argentines; humanitarianism remained at the core of the British attitude.

Medical organisation

The high level of casualties meant that the British military medical services faced their greatest challenge for 30 years. Like the rest of the armed forces, their operational parameters were largely set by the fact that all medical services had to be self-sufficient, there being no proximate land-based hospital for the evacuation of serious casualties. Later in the conflict, Uruguay offered Montevideo as

The British medical units and facilities in and around the Falklands can be organised according to whether they were based offshore or on land. Supply for all units came from the tri-service Defence Medical Equipment Depot at Ludgershall, Wiltshire. In overall command of the medical service for the Falklands was RN Surgeon Commander Rick Jolly, who commanded the Medical Squadron of the Commando Logistics Regiment.

Offshore medical facilities

Offshore, the most extensive of the medical facilities was the hospital ship *Uganda*. The SS *Uganda* had been requisitioned in the Mediterranean, the liner having been mid-voyage with a passenger list consisting mainly of schoolchildren. It was designated as a hospital ship and its conversion into that role was largely accomplished in just 65 hours, at the British naval base in Gibraltar. Adaptations included turning the children's veranda into an operating theatre and the smoke room into an intensive care ward. The ship also had to be fitted with the mechanical means to produce its own fresh water, for drinking and cleaning.

The *Uganda* would be the first British hospital ship in operation since HMS *Maine*, which had been deployed back in the days of the Korean War. Its onboard facilities included:

- 135-strong medical team (led by Surgeon Captain A.J. Rintoul. This figure included 24 RM bandsmen who would act as stretcher-bearers)
- 250 hospital beds
- Operating theatre
- Intensive Care Unit
- High-Dependency Care Ward
- Climate-controlled Burns Unit.

Although *Uganda* was by far the largest floating medical facility, it was not the only ship with casualty responsibilities. In support of the converted liner were three hospital ships, used for receiving casualties from onshore fighting, providing them with advanced front-line treatment while transferring them to *Uganda* or up to Montevideo. These ships were *Hecla*, *Hydra* and *Herald*, all Royal Navy survey vessels. Together *Uganda* and the hospital ships formed what was known as the 'Red Cross Box', a zone to the north of San Carlos Water designated as a receiving area for casualties.

It should also be noted that *Canberra* was originally selected as a hospital ship conversion, at least in part, alongside its role as a troop transport. This was mainly due to the fact that the bulk of the Task Force's combat medical teams (described in the following section) were to be sailing on the ship; once the other troops

had been offloaded, some medical staff could remain on board the ship to treat casualties. Ultimately, *Uganda* took the primary role of hospital ship during the conflict, although *Canberra* did receive a total of some 170 casualties.

On-land units and the treatment process

Deployed initially as the medical support for 3 Cdo Bde (although they provided cross-service casualty evacuation and treatment), were the following medical units:

- Commando Medical Squadron
- 2 × RN Surgical Support Teams (SSTs)
- Parachute Clearing Troop (an airborne medical team working in support of 2 Para; part of 16 Field Ambulance RAMC)
- 2 × Field Surgical Teams (FSTs).

Under the umbrella of 5 Bde were:

- 16 Field Ambulance RAMC (minus the Parachute Clearing Troop)
- 2 × FSTs.

While there were extensive medical facilities offshore, it was naturally imperative that a structured system of treatment was established at front-line and rear-area levels also. Whenever a casualty was taken, the most immediate treatment for the wounded individual was by the soldier next to him. All British Army

ABOVE A wounded soldier is taken from a Sea King helicopter to a field hospital for emergency treatment.
(Defence Picture Library)

leaving as many combat troops as possible on the front line.) The RAPs, which included a military surgeon (the Regimental Medical Officer), were mobile stations that were not designed to house patients for more than just a few hours; they were part of the network designed to transit casualties upwards through ever-more-sophisticated medical treatment. Thus their main job was basically to keep people alive before they could be taken out by helicopter to higher levels of care. They were also busy places, as explained in this passage from an article by A.R. Marsh in the *Journal of the Royal Society of Medicine*, written a year after the conflict:

> Surgeon Lt R. Adley and Lt Colonel A. Warsop gave accounts of their experiences as RMOs with 42 Commando and 2nd Battalion Scots Guards. During the 31-day period it was ashore, including the advance on Mount Kent, the Marine RAP received 114 casualties. Thirty-six were treated and returned to duty, and the rest, including 24 wounded in action, were evacuated rearward. The others were non-battle injuries and many had trench foot.[1]

ABOVE A sobering place – the rudimentary morgue at San Carlos, manned by Paras and Marines. *(Defence Picture Library)*

BELOW A view of the ASU at Ajax Bay, formerly a refrigeration plant, taken from out on San Carlos Water. *(Andy Cole)*

personnel had basic first-aid training, which was refreshed significantly during the journey from the UK to the Falklands. As a standard part of their medical pack, each soldier carried a shell dressing for packing open wounds, plus a morphine syrette for pain control. More advance life-saving treatment would then be provided within minutes by the company medics, either in the field or at a Company Aid Post. Once the medics had stabilised the casualty within their available means, they arranged for his transfer to a Regimental Aid Post (RAP), which was part of each battalion's headquarters unit. (Note that up to this point individuals such as bandsmen, cooks and HQ personnel were acting as stretcher-bearers,

If the severity of the wounds now warranted it, the next stop for the casualty was typically one of the Advanced Surgical Units (ASUs), the biggest of which was initially at Ajax Bay; it was established following the San Carlos landings. Just prior to the landings, the second-line medical treatment role was given to small teams aboard *Canberra*, *Norland* and *Sir Galahad*. The Ajax Bay facility was a very active field hospital, set up in an abandoned refrigeration plant. Conditions inside the building tested the professionalism of the medical services to the limit. There was no running water, electricity or ventilation; all such basic services had to be provided by engineers. In cold, dark and sometimes insanitary conditions, therefore, the ASU team had to perform every conceivable type of combat injury treatment. From 21 May to 9 June, the facility saw 725 patients, and performed 210 surgeries under general anaesthetic. Not only that, but the ASU was also squarely in a war zone, and was bombed and shelled on several occasions, with casualties being taken actually within

the medical station. Two unexploded bombs remained embedded in the ASU, simply packed with sandbags and stoically ignored.

As the land campaign on the Falklands expanded and shifted its weight inexorably towards Stanley, the Ajax Bay ASU came to be supplemented by two Advanced Dressing Stations (ADSs), which performed some similar functions to the ASU (which also functioned as the main ADS on the Falklands). One ADS was established at Teal Inlet by 1 FST, and provided medical support to 3 Cdo, while the other was at Fitzroy for 5 Bde, established by 16 Field Ambulance. All of the main medical stations came to have Wessex CASEVAC helicopters assigned to them; by the time of the Port Stanley assault, the Teal Inlet and Fitzroy facilities each had three helicopters assigned, such was the intensity of the combat. In total, 108 major operations were performed at Teal Inlet, Fitzroy and aboard SS *Uganda*. For those who were so seriously injured that repatriation to the UK was the only option, their journey would typically be from SS *Uganda* via hospital ship to Montevideo, by RAF VC-10 from Montevideo to Ascension Island, then from Ascension Island to the UK also by VC-10.

Medical lessons

One of the most impressive factors about the British military medical services during the Falklands War was that there was an almost 100% survival rate for wounded soldiers once they found themselves in the evacuation and treatment system. In large part this was due to two factors: 1) the sheer skill and experience of the medical teams and 2) the speed of transfer from incurring the wound to arriving on a surgeon's table. The latter was especially important. As a rule, most serious casualties went from the battlefield to an ASU/ADS, or to *Uganda*, in under 45 minutes. This timeline was affected by some external factors, particularly the availability of helicopters. During the later stages of the campaign, for example, when the British forces were incurring heavy casualties on the approaches to Stanley, all parts of the evacuation chain – but particularly helicopter CASEVAC – were overstretched, made worse by the fact that most of the helicopters could

not fly during the night hours, when several key battles were fought. (Some helicopter crews did have night-vision technology, but it was only available in limited numbers.) Because of this, the casualty evacuation times did become extended, even up to 12 hours (the worst case of a transfer to Ajax Bay from the battlefield was three days), but overall such lengths of time were the exception, not the rule.

Throughout the war, the medical teams had to adjust to certain patterns of injury, depending on the type of combat under way. As a very rough rule, land combat brought a high percentage of penetrating wounds – bullets and shell fragments being the primary causes – plus some blast injuries, while the fighting at sea resulted in a

WORKING ON *UGANDA*

Nicci Pugh joined the Royal Navy as a QARNNS nurse in 1979, and served aboard the *Uganda* during the Falklands War. Here she recounts some of her experiences:

The Uganda *had been requisitioned in Alexandria from P&O Cruises, who used her as an educational cruise vessel. She needed to be converted into a hospital ship of 500 to 600 beds.*

Three days after we were all summoned on board, we sailed out of port, frantically building and assembling and flat-packing, only finishing the conversion the day we arrived at the Task Force Base in Ascension. It took 10 days and we were flat out the entire time.

Most of us believed, and hoped, that it was an exercise; a serious one, but a situation that would be resolved politically. But soon after leaving Ascension, heading south towards the Falklands, we heard that HMS Sheffield *had been sunk – the first Royal Navy ship sunk in action since World War Two – and we all knew our services were now urgently required.*

We were to position north of the Total Exclusion Zone. Initially we never intended to enter it but by the time we arrived, we just proceeded into it and almost at once, received our first patients: very severely burned survivors from Sheffield *who had been in the sick bay on HMS* Hermes *before an RN Sea King helicopter could transfer them safely across.*

Of all the many pieces of equipment used to convert the ship, one stands out as being utterly crucial: our steel helicopter landing pad. It allowed us to evacuate patients directly from other ships and from the battlefield. And that reduction in time spent in casualty evacuation saved many, many lives.

We soon established a routine: by daylight, we'd enter Falkland Sound to collect casualties from the dressing stations set up ashore; but the Geneva Convention obliges hospital ships to be fully illuminated from dusk to dawn – lit up like a Christmas tree – making us a beacon for enemy aircraft, and obliging us to sail out of the zone until the next day. Later we were able to stay put in Grantham Sound.

Most wounds were caused by shrapnel, mortar or bullets, new to most of us NHS-trained nurses, but a fellow theatre sister had worked during the Troubles in the Royal Victoria, Belfast, and I'd worked in major trauma units, so we were able to train our nurses as we went along.

There were usually two operating teams working at one time: we had to adapt and innovate as much as we could. The South Atlantic Ocean is notoriously windy, so with the ship moving up and down, we had to find ways to restrain our instruments and anaesthetic machines.

The theatre was midships for increased stability, and the merchant navy officers on the bridge had a telephone connected to us, and when necessary I would relay messages to the bridge asking for the ship to be turned into the wind temporarily, so a delicate piece of surgery could be done.

We were working extremely hard, particularly after the sinking of the Sir Galahad, *and the whole ship's personnel were on full alert to expect a lot of burns cases. It was a frenetic, exhausting time, split into watches for 24-hour care. And after the surrender, when casualties could be brought in much more safely, that was a very busy time too.*[2]

high percentage of burn casualties. In total, penetrating injuries constituted 52.3% of the total injuries, while burns were 21.6%. But as well as the combat wounds, the medics also saw a significant percentage of environmental injuries, especially trench foot, which constituted a worrying 13.6% of the total injuries. The Surgeon Commander F. St C. Golden later described what he saw of trench foot in Royal Marines:

> *In summary then, all experienced cold wet feet for most of the 24 days of the campaign. Numbness began to develop after about 7–10 days. At night, in their sleeping bags, the numbness would be replaced by paraesthesia, or pain, or both – described by some like electric shocks running up the legs from their toes. In some cases this pain was severe enough to keep them awake. On weight-bearing in the morning, the pain was sometimes almost unbearable for the initial 5 or 10 minutes, but would then gradually wane and once again be replaced by numbness on re-exposure to cold. Some – particularly those with very severe nocturnal pain – found their feet had swollen to such a degree in the morning that they had difficulty in putting on their boots; or if it had been necessary for them to sleep with their boots on, they had difficulty in tying their laces. The 70 most severe cases were transferred to the hospital ship* Uganda. *The majority, however, out of a sense of loyalty to their comrades and a desire to be 'in at the kill', persevered with remarkable fortitude, although some were hobbling at the end. It is considered that enlisted men would not have continued under these conditions.*[3]

In addition to trench foot, another problem encountered was that of diarrhoea and vomiting, caused by living in insanitary field conditions.

Blood supply was a logistical concern for the Task Force medics, hence it was sourced in very large volumes – a total of 3,262 units were collected, nearly 800 units coming from the Army Blood Supply Depot in the UK, while much of the remainder was locally collected aboard the ships during the passage down to the Falklands. Ultimately, however, only 605 units of blood were actually used, the prewar casualty predictions being higher than actual numbers incurred. Nevertheless, post-conflict analysis found that the unique storage requirements of blood stocks, which typically had a maximum shelf life of 28 days, meant that the blood was scattered among the fleet in refrigerators, with many of the units going out of date or simply not being in the right place at the right time to transfer to casualties. Greater centralisation of blood stocks was therefore a post-war recommendation for future operations.

In general, the medical services on the Falklands performed extremely well. Hence the 1983 *Journal of the Royal Society of Medicine* article on the Falklands War, already quoted above, noted that 'There were few new medical lessons learned during the Falklands conflict, but many old ones were relearned and their values reinforced. In particular, the value of physical fitness in troops and training in first-aid were underlined. These two factors more than anything else helped to minimise casualties and mortality.'[4]

BELOW An injured soldier from the battle at Goose Green is ferried from a Scout helicopter to the ASU at Ajax Bay. *(Defence Picture Library)*

BELOW RIGHT The late Surgeon-Captain Richard 'Rick' Jolly OBE, Officer Commanding Medical Squadron of the Commando Logistics Regiment, Royal Marines, who headed the establishment of the 'Red and Green Life Machine' in Ajax Bay. *(Defence Picture Library)*

ABOVE The ASU established at Ajax Bay was hit by several Argentine bombs; here we can see the damage done to the galley end by one of the attacks. *(Andy Cole)*

BELOW Military doctors and surgeons at work in the Ajax Bay ASU; note the generally poor quality of the lighting under which they worked. *(Defence Picture Library)*

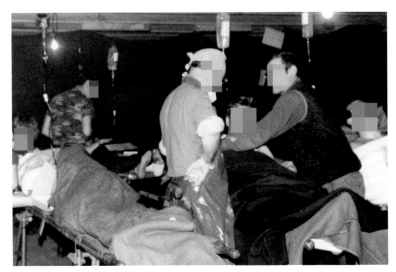

Glossary of abbreviations

AA	anti-aircraft
AAC	Army Air Corps
AAM	air-to-air missile
AAR	air-to-air refuelling
ADS	Advanced Dressing Station
ASM	air-to-surface missile
ASU	Advanced Surgical Unit
ASW	Anti-Submarine Warfare
ATGW	anti-tank guided weapon
BAOR	British Army of the Rhine
BAS	British Antarctic Survey
BFSUAI	British Forces Support Unit in Ascension Island
CAP	Combat Air Patrol
CAS	Close Air Support
CASEVAC	casualty evacuation
CBU	Cluster Bomb Unit
CLOS	command line-of-sight
CVBG	Carrier Battle Group
DSCS	Defense Satellite Communications System (US)
EOD	Explosive Ordnance Disposal
FAA	Fleet Air Arm
FAO	Forward Air Observer
FBMA	Forward Brigade Maintenance Area
FIDF	Falkland Islands Defence Force
FST	Field Surgical Team
HDS	Helicopter Delivery Service
LGB	Laser-Guided Bombs

LPD	Landing Platform Dock
M&AWC	Mountain & Arctic Warfare Cadre
MARTSU	Mobile Aircraft Repair Transport and Salvage Unit
MEZ	Maritime Exclusion Zone (MEZ)
NAS	Naval Air Squadron
NGS	Naval Gunfire Support
OP	observation post
PGM	Precision Guided Munition
RAF	Royal Air Force
RAMC	Royal Army Medical Corps
RAP	Regimental Aid Post
RE	Royal Engineers
RFA	Royal Fleet Auxiliary
RM	Royal Marines
RN	Royal Navy
SACLOS	semi-automatic command to line-of-sight
SAM	surface-to-air missile
SAR	Search and Rescue
SAS	Special Air Service
SBS	Special Boat Service
SCOT	Satellite Communications Onboard Terminal
SF	Special Forces
SST	Surgical Support Team
TEZ	Total Exclusion Zone
V/STOL	Vertical/Short Take-Off and Landing
VERTREP	Vertical Replenishment

Endnotes

Introduction
1 Nott 1981: 4
2 Nott 1981: 9
3 Nott 1981: 10

Chapter 1
1 Southby-Tailyour 1983: viii–ix
2 Van der Bijl 1999: 17
3 Van der Bijl 1999: 25 and 27

Chapter 2
1 Margaret Thatcher, House of Commons: 2 April 1982
2 UN Security Council Resolution 502: 2 April 1982
3 Privratsky 2014: n.p.
4 Johnson-Allen 2011: 20
5 Marshall Cavendish 1983: 57

Chapter 3
1 Burgoyne 2007: 21–22
2 Chant 2001: 47
3 Flight Lieutenant David Morgan; transcript of interview at https://www.youtube.com/watch?v=3Vg2RTXZmoY; used with permission
4 British Operational Research Branch Report 1982; quoted in Lee Richards 'Examination of Argentine Air Effort – Arcre' https://arcre.com/falklands/argaireffort Accessed December 2017

Chapter 4
1 Department of the Navy 1983: 4
2 https://www.theguardian.com/uk-news/2017/oct/15/revealed-full-story-behind-sinking-of-falklands-warship-hms-sheffield
3 Admiralty Board of Inquiry, Loss of HMS *Sheffield*, Annex A, 22 July 1982: A-1–A-2
4 Hart Dyke 2007: 148
5 Hart Dyke 2007: 150–51
6 Badsey 2005: 205–06
7 Marshall Cavendish 1983: 150

Chapter 5
1 Freedman 2005: 723–35
2 Vaux 1986: 177

Chapter 6
1 Van der Bijl 1999: 68
2 Privratsky 2014: n.p.

Chapter 7
1 Quoted in Middlebrook 2001: 275
2 Quoted in Marshall Editions 1983: 325
3 Quoted in Marshall Editions 1983: 328

Chapter 8
1 Marsh 1983: 978
2 Pugh 2017: http://www.britishlegion.org.uk/community/stories/general/our-services-were-urgently-required-a-qarnns-nurse-remembers-the-falklands-war/
3 Quoted in Marsh 1983: 979–80
4 Marsh 1983: 981

Select bibliography and further reading

Badsey, Stephen, Rob Havers and Mark Grove (2005). *The Falklands Conflict Twenty Years On: Lessons for the Future*. Abingdon: Routledge

Burden, R., M. Draper, D. Rough, C. Smith and D. Wilton (1986). *Falklands: The Air War*. Twickenham: British Aviation Research Group

Burgoyne, Harry (2007). 'The First Operational C-130 Air-to-Air Refuel in the South Atlantic', *Spirit of the Air*, Vol. 2, No. 4, 2007

Chant, Christopher (2001). *Air War in the Falklands 1982*. Oxford: Osprey Publishing

Foster, Simon (1995). *Hit the Beach! Amphibious Warfare from the Plains of Abraham to San Carlos Water*. London: Arms & Armour

Freedman, Sir Lawrence (2005). *The Official History of the Falklands Campaign*, Vol II. Abingdon: Routledge

Hart Dyke, David (2007). *Four Weeks in May: The Loss of HMS* Coventry – *A Captain's Story*. London: Atlantic Books

Hastings, Max and Simon Jenkins (1997). *The Battle for the Falklands*. London: Pan Books

Hezsely, Lt Col Csaba B. (1988). *Argentine Air Power in the Falklands War*. Maxwell AFB: Air War College

Johnson-Allen, John (2011). *They Couldn't Have Done It Without Us: The Merchant Navy in the Falklands War*. Rendlesham: Seafarer Books

Loss of HMS *Sheffield* Board of Inquiry report, 1983–84

Marsh, A.R. (1983). 'A Short but Distant War – the Falklands Campaign', *Journal of the Royal Society of Medicine*, Vol. 76, November

Marshall Editions (1983). *The Falklands War* (collected partwork). London: Marshall Cavendish

Middlebrook, Martin (2001). *The Falklands War 1982*. London: Penguin

Privratsky, Kenneth L. (2014). *Logistics in the Falklands War*. Barnsley: Pen & Sword

Pugh, Nicci (2010). *White Ship, Red Crosses: A Nursing Memoir of the Falklands War*. Ely: Melrose Books

Report of a Committee of Privy Counsellors (January 1983). *Falkland Islands Review*. London: HMSO

Secretary of State for Defence (June 1981). *The United Kingdom Defence Programme: The Way Forward*. London: HMSO

Smith, Gordon (2006). *Battle Atlas of the Falklands War*. Penarth: Naval-History.Net

Southby-Tailyour, Ewen (1985). *Falkland Island Shores*. London: Conway Maritime

Thompson, Julian (2009). *3 Commando Brigade in the Falklands: No Picnic*. Barnsley: Pen & Sword

US Department of the Navy (February 1983). *Lessons of the Falklands: Summary Report*. Washington DC: Department of the Navy

Van der Bijl, Nicholas (1999). *Nine Battles to Stanley*. London: Leo Cooper

Vaux, Nick (1986). *Take That Hill*. Washington, DC: Pergamon-Brassey's International Defense Publishers

Ward, Commander 'Sharkey' (1992). *Sea Harrier over the Falklands: A Maverick at War*. Barnsley: Leo Cooper

White, Rowland (2007). *Vulcan 607*. London: Corgi

Index